Phonics

Phonics

Practice, research and policy

Edited by
Maureen Lewis and Sue Ellis

Paul Chapman
Publishing

Paul Chapman Publishing
A SAGE Publications Company
1 Oliver's Yard
55 City Road
London EC1Y 1SP

SAGE Publications Inc
2455 Teller Road
Thousand Oaks, California 91320

SAGE Publications India Pvt Ltd
B-42, Panchsheel Enclave
Post Box 4109
New Delhi 110 017

Library of Congress Control Number: 2006902801
A catalogue record for this book is available from the British Library

ISBN-10 1-4129-3085-5   ISBN-13 978-1-4129-3085-7
ISBN-10 1-4129-3086-3   ISBN-13 978-1-4129-3086-4 (pbk)

Typeset by C&M Digitals (P) Ltd., Chennai, India
Printed on paper from sustainable resources
Printed and bound in Great Britain by Athenaeum Press Ltd Gateshead, Tyne & Wear

Contents

Contributors

Jennifer Chew is a retired teacher of English to students aged 16-plus. It was the spelling problems of these students, many of whom were academically very able, which led her to become interested in the way that beginners were taught to read and spell, and to realize that the methods used in Britain from at least the 1960s onwards had under-emphasized the teaching of the alphabetic code. Since 2004, she has edited the newsletter of the UK chapter of the Reading Reform Foundation, an organization which was formed in 1989 to campaign for phonics teaching to be restored to its proper place.

Moya Cove is a lecturer in the Faculty of Education at the University of Glasgow where she teaches on a range of undergraduate and postgraduate courses in teacher education. She has worked in partnership with a number of Scottish education authorities to support national and local literacy initiatives and with the Scottish curriculum body (Learning and Teaching Scotland) to develop national curriculum support materials. Her research interests include the area of early literacy development, formative assessment, early years provision and teacher education.

Henrietta Dombey is Professor Emeritus of Literacy in Primary Education at the University of Brighton. Since the start of her teaching career, when she was confronted with a class of 7-year-olds with very little purchase on written English, she has been passionately interested in the teaching of reading. This interest has encompassed attention to phonics, children's knowledge of the syntax and semantics of written language and the interactions between teachers, children and texts that appear to be productive of literacy learning.

Sue Ellis was a primary teacher in London before joining Strathclyde University. She is currently a Reader in Childhood and Primary Studies and her main work involves research, teaching and consultancy in the fields of language, literacy and children's literature. Her publications speak to teachers, policymakers and researchers, although her main research interests are in the development of children as writers and in the pedagogies of home and school. She teaches students on all four years of the B.Ed degree and also works with qualified teachers on continuing professional development.

Sally Evans is a Key Stage 1 teacher and works in a London primary school. She is subject leader for literacy and is fascinated by children's literacy development as they move through the primary years.

Sandra Farmer is Senior Teacher Adviser in Lancashire, with particular responsibility for Primary English and SpLD (Dyslexia) – from Early Years through to Further Education. She has taught in a variety of schools – secondary, primary and also in the arena of special education since 1970. Recently she edited *English Four to Eleven* on behalf of the United Kingdom Literacy Association (UKLA).

Prue Goodwin works part time at the University of Reading and spends the rest her time working freelance for schools, LEAs and children's publishers. She has published several books including *The Literate Classroom* (2000), which she edited, and *Teaching Language and Literacy in the Early Years* (2002), which she co-authored with Margaret Perkins.

Kathy Hall is Professor of Education at the Open University. She researches in the areas of literacy, assessment and classroom interaction and her work has been published in numerous journal articles and book chapters. She is the author of *Listening to Stephen Read: Multiple Perspectives on Literacy* (2003b) and *Literacy and Schooling: Towards Renewal in Primary Education Policy* (2004). She has directed a number of research projects and is currently completing a project on rural childhoods in the Republic of Ireland. She is president elect of the United Kingdom Literacy Association (UKLA).

Laura Huxford was director of professional development in the National Literacy Strategy in England, where she was responsible for the production of materials for teachers on phonics and spelling: *Progression in Phonics* (DfEE, 1999a) *Playing with Sounds* (DfES, 2003a) and *Year 2 and Year 3 Planning Exemplification and Spelling Programme* (DfES, 2003b). Her background is in primary teaching, teacher training and research into children's developing ability to read and spell. She is currently Senior Research Fellow at the University of Oxford investigating the development of children's oral language.

Maureen Lewis is an independent education consultant and Honorary Research Fellow at the University of Exeter. She has been a primary teacher, university researcher and lecturer and a regional director for the National Literacy Strategy (NLS). She has published many books, articles and classroom materials and authored several of the NLS training materials. She is currently involved in an action research project with a group of leading literacy teachers, investigating how teachers can support the development of reading comprehension.

Lyndsay Macnair is Deputy Headteacher at St Ninians Primary School in Stirling; she has taught across Central Scotland, England and New Zealand. She has responsibility for Early Years but has a particular interest in Pre-school. She is currently developing a *Documentation approach to learning* within the school nursery in conjunction with Stirling Council. She is actively involved in promoting enterprise within the school and taking it into the community. Her work in this area has recently been highlighted in a case study published by Learning and Teaching Scotland.

Elspeth McCartney lectures in the Division of Speech and Language Therapy, Educational and Professional Studies Department, University of Strathclyde, on speech and language disorders in children. She holds qualifications as both a teacher and a speech and language therapist, and has published extensively on speech and language therapists and teachers working together. Her research field is language therapy for children with language impairment in schools.

Jackie Marsh is Reader in Education at the University of Sheffield, where she is involved in teaching on masters and doctoral programmes in literacy and early childhood education. Her research is focused on young children's use of popular culture, media and digital literacy in homes, schools and early years settings. She is currently President of the United Kingdom Literacy Association (UKLA).

Margaret Perkins lectures in literacy education at the University of Reading, where she is the course director for the Primary Graduate Teacher Programme. She is co-author of *Teaching Language and Literacy in the Early Years* (Goodwin and Perkins, 2002).

Michael Rosen is a well-known poet, writer and broadcaster. He published his first children's book in 1974 and continues to write best-selling books and poetry for children. His wide-ranging interest in literature and literacy includes presenting BBC radio's *Word of Mouth* and hosting *Reading Aloud* on Teachers' Television. He is a visiting lecturer on children's literature at London Metropolitan University.

Vivienne Smith lectures at Strathclyde University in the Department of Childhood and Primary Studies. She is interested in the development of children as readers, and especially in how they interpret text and make it meaningful.

Jonathan Solity is a lecturer in Educational Psychology and Honorary Research Fellow at University College London. He has led a number of research projects into the most effective ways of teaching literacy and maths to raise attainment and prevent learning difficulties. He has written six books and numerous articles on the psychology of teaching and learning, psychological assessment and the teaching of reading and maths.

Rhona Stainthorp is a Professor of Education in the School of Psychology at the Institute of Education, University of London. She has been involved with teacher education at all levels for the last 30 years. Her research interests are in the psychology of reading and writing development including spelling and handwriting. She believes passionately that knowledge of the research evidence from cognitive and developmental psychologists about the development of reading should be part of the training of all primary teachers.

John Stannard has spent his professional life in primary education as a teacher, teacher trainer, local authority adviser and inspector. He joined Her Majesty's Inspectorate in 1986 and later, as Ofsted's specialist English adviser, set up the National Literacy Project in 18 under-performing LEAs. Subsequently, he designed and directed the National Literacy Strategy for five years, retiring in 2000. Since then he has worked as an international consultant for CfBT, an independent company, advising and supporting governments on national strategies for raising standards in the Caribbean, South-East Asia, the Middle East and Canada. He is visiting Professor at the University of Southampton, Department of Education and, in 2000, was awarded a CBE for services to education.

Morag Stuart is Professor of the Psychology of Reading at the Institute of Education in London. She spent some 16 years teaching children in Key Stage 1, and therefore was delighted to discover, when she started a part-time evening degree course in psychology at Birkbeck College in the mid-1970s, that there were research psychologists who devoted their working lives to investigating what is involved in reading the words on the page. Prior to this she had no idea why some children learned to do this almost without teaching and others struggled, however hard she tried to teach them. She began her own research into the development of word reading skills in the early 1980s, and continues to find this a fascinating topic.

David Wray taught in primary schools for 10 years and is currently Professor of Literacy Education at the University of Warwick. He has published over 30 books on aspects of literacy teaching and is best known for his work on developing teaching strategies to help pupils access the curriculum through literacy.

Dominic Wyse is a lecturer in Early Years and Primary Education at the University of Cambridge with a specialism in the teaching of English, language and literacy. His work in the last few years has particularly focused on the extent to which the pedagogy of the National Literacy Strategy is informed by evidence. His most recent research article looked at the teaching of grammar and pupils' word choices, and was published in 2006 in the Cambridge Journal of Education. His most recent book is *The Good Writing Guide for Education Students* (2006).

UKLA

The United Kingdom Literacy Association

UKLA is a registered charity, which has as its sole object the advancement of education in literacy. UKLA is concerned with literacy education in school and out-of- school settings in all phases of education and members include classroom teachers, teaching assistants, school literacy co-ordinators, LEA literacy consultants, teacher educators, researchers, inspectors, advisors, publishers and librarians.

The Association was founded in 1963 as the United Kingdom Reading Association. In 2003 it changed its name to the United Kingdom Literacy Association in order to reflect more accurately its wider range of concerns. Through the work of its various committees and Special Interest Groups, the Association is active in a wide variety of areas, both nationally and internationally. UKLA works with a range of government and non-governmental agencies on issues of national interest. The Association is also committed to the funding and dissemination of high-quality national and international research projects that include practitioner- researchers.

UKLA provides a forum for discussion and debate, together with information and inspiration. We do this through our wide range of conferences- international, national, regional and local – and our publications, which include a professional magazine, 'English 4-11', and two journals, 'Literacy' and the 'Journal of Research in Reading'. This series of co-published titles with Sage Publications complements our range of in – house publications and provides a further opportunity to disseminate the high quality and vibrant work of the association. In order to find out more about UKLA, including details about membership, see our website: http://www.ukla.org

Introduction
Phonics: The Wider Picture

Maureen Lewis and Sue Ellis

Learning to read is a vital foundation to becoming a literate, educated person. Reading offers opportunities for enjoyment, for increasing our knowledge of the world and for enhancing our imagination and creativity. It also gives people access to improved life chances – success or failure in becoming a reader is a strong indicator of future progress in school and beyond.

Throughout the developed world therefore governments are giving great priority to literacy and are asking schools to ensure that children reach certain standards of reading achievement. In England, for example, this is manifest in the ever-increasing targets set for the number of children reaching the expected reading level for their age group as measured by national tests. In America the *No child left behind* legislation focuses on literacy teaching and pupil literacy achievement, again measuring children's performance with state-administered tests. In Australia the government has recently concluded a *National Inquiry into the Teaching of Literacy* (DEST, 2004) and has called for higher standards of literacy through a set of 'National Goals'. In the developed world, ensuring high levels of literacy is a priority and there are ambitious plans to support the developing world in achieving the same goal. The United Nations has made the pledge that by 2015 all the world's children will complete primary schooling and UNESCO has nominated 2003–2012 as the *United Nations' Literacy Decade*. Literacy is recognized not only as important for the personal development and life chances of individuals but also as vital to the spiritual, cultural and economic wellbeing of nations.

Given the central importance of literacy in our developed and developing world, it is no surprise therefore that we want to know 'How best can children be enabled to learn to read and write?' To try to answer this quesion there has been an *Independent Review of the Teaching of Early Reading* (DfES, 2006) – hereafter called the Rose Review – in England. A similar review has been undertaken in Australia – *Teaching Reading: Report and Recommendations* (DEST, 2005) – and in the United States, the National Reading Panel was set up in 1997 to investigate the research about the teaching of reading (NRP, 2000b). We will return to these reports later.

This perennial question – How best can children be enabled to learn to read and write? – has been asked for many decades. It continues to be asked because there is no simple answer and because what we know about how children learn to read and write changes over time. In the last decade or so there has been a fairly widespread consensus on the elements of a successful reading programme. This consensus view has recognized the importance of phonics as a reading strategy, but has seen this as one strategy among several that a reader might use within the context of a rich and broad literacy curriculum. The Australian reading report, for example, concluded that:

> The evidence is clear . . . that direct systematic instruction in phonics during the early years of schooling is an essential foundation for teaching children to read. Findings from the research evidence indicate that all students learn best when teachers adopt an integrated approach to reading that explicitly teaches phonemic awareness, phonics, fluency, vocabulary knowledge and comprehension. This approach, coupled with effective support from the child's home, is critical to success. (DEST, 2005: 11)

It went on to recommend that:

> . . . teachers provide systematic, direct and explicit phonics instruction so that children master the essential alphabetic code-breaking skills required for foundational reading proficiency. Equally, that teachers provide an integrated approach to reading that supports the development of oral language, vocabulary, grammar, reading fluency, comprehension and the literacies of new technologies. (DEST, 2005: 14, Recommendation 2)

This 'phonics as part of a wider approach' is often expressed as 'phonics is necessary, but not sufficient'. In the first two chapters of this book, Kathy Hall and Morag Stuart explore this view. Hall argues that learning to read is influenced by many different factors, including such things as children's understanding of the pleasures and purposes of reading, the range of skills children need to be taught and employ (including phonics), parental and societal influences and teacher expertise. She goes on to argue that phonics is important in learning to read but it is not the only important element. This chapter reflects the views of the United Kingdom Literacy Association, which held a series of members' meetings during 2005 to discuss the role of phonics in the teaching of reading. In the second chapter, Morag Stuart sharpens the focus to look closely at why phonics is important in learning to read, and argues that not only does it support the beginning of reading but that it offers readers the opportunity to develop independent 'self-teaching' strategies.

That phonics is neccessary in learning to read is not therefore at the heart of the current debate about the role of phonics. Rather, over the last few years the debate has centred on:

- whether children are being taught phonics/enough phonics;
- what form of phonics (synthetic or analytic) should be used;
- the systematic teaching of phonics;
- when best to teach phonics; and
- how fast to pace it.

Are children being taught phonics?

Throughout the 1970s and 1980s there was heated debate as to whether phonics should be taught as part of the early reading curriculum. Such disputes about the role of phonics have a long history. Moya Cove's chapter, 'Sounds Familiar', traces the development of phonics teaching and the arguments around this. Cove's 'long view' helps us to see these issues from a wider perspective. The introduction of the National Literacy Strategy (NLS) in England in 1998 gave a strong impetus in that country for the explicit teaching of phonics to children from the age of five. The *Framework for Teaching* (DfEE, 1998a) contains 'phonological awareness, phonics and spelling' objectives from reception year (5-year-olds) onwards. The NLS suggests that about 15 minutes of the daily literacy hour is devoted to daily teaching of this 'word level' strand. As part of the introduction of the NLS, all teachers received training and the second (and largest) module of the National Literacy Strategy's *Literacy Training Pack* (DfEE, 1998b) focused on subject knowledge about phonics. A related issue to the phonics training that practising teachers were offered was debate about the knowledge of phonics that trainee teachers needed. In Scotland and America, it is not specified. In England, the standards for initial teacher training institutions contained an explicit section on the phonic knowledge that trainee teachers had to demonstrate in order to complete their course successfully. The Rose Review continues this approach by recommending a strengthening of the phonics training teachers and trainees receive.

Following the introduction of the NLS, *Progression in Phonics* (DfEE, 1999a) was published to give teachers a practical and systematic phonics teaching programme. This was sent to all English primary schools. The thrust of government policy was clear: phonics should be taught and teachers needed specific subject knowledge to do this. As a measure of this policy, three years later in *Teaching of Phonics: A paper by HMI*, Ofsted reported that:

> Phonics teaching has increased significantly since the implementation of the National Literacy Strategy. The debate is no longer about whether phonic knowledge and skills should be taught, but how best to teach them. (Ofsted, 2001: 2)

By 2005, Ofsted were more detailed in their comments about 'how best to teach them':

> . . . inspection evidence continues to show significant variation in the effectiveness with which pupils are taught the phonic knowledge they need to decode text. In the schools with high standards phonics was *taught early*, *systematically* and *rapidly* so that pupils quickly gained the ability to decode text (and begin to write too), associating letters with sounds. Where standards were lower, expectations as to the speed at which pupils could acquire phonic knowledge were insufficient and the phonics teaching lacked systematic or full coverage of sounds and their combinations. (Ofsted, 2005: para. 42, our italics)

This statement was part of a growing pressure to look more closely at exactly *how* phonics was taught, and mirrored similar questions raised in Australia,

New Zealand and the United States. In Australia, for example, an open letter to the government signed by 26 Australian psychologists and reading researchers raised such issues (DEST, 2005: 2). Chapter 10, 'Responses to Rose', considers this 'growing pressure' in England and gives commentators with different stances on the role of phonics in reading an opportunity to comment on the Rose Review.

Different approaches to phonics teaching – synthetic and analytic phonics

In the debate on the role and teaching of phonics, advocates of a 'synthetic phonics only' approach (see, for example, Chew, 1997; Miskin, 2003) argue that the results obtained by such programmes are far in advance of those obtained by children using a mixed phonics programme (synthetic and analytic) or a mixed strategy approach (phonics as one of several reading 'searchlights'). We will examine these claims, but first we must define the differences between synthetic and analytic phonics.

In synthetic phonics programmes, children are systematically taught the phonemes (sounds) associated with particular graphemes (letters). Children begin from hearing the phonemes in a spoken word and blending phonemes orally. In reading, individual phonemes are recognized from the grapheme, pronounced and blended together (synthesized) to create the word. For example, when encountering an unknown single-syllable word such as *h/e/n* the child would sound out its three phonemes and then blend them together to form *hen*. Blending is seen as a very important skill. The skill of segmenting words into phonemes for spelling is also taught, and blending and segmenting are introduced as reversible processes. The order in which new phonemes are introduced and the speed at which this is undertaken are important (see following section). Synthetic phonics programmes emphasize decodable words and some proponents do not favour teaching other reading strategies or an initial sight vocabulary of high-frequency, non-phonically regular words in the early stages of beginning a synthetic phonics programme.

In analytic phonics, children identify phonemes in whole words and are encouraged to segment the words into phonemes. They also analyse similar characteristics in other words (for example, hen, house, hill all begin with the same sound; tin, sin, win, pin all share the same medial and end phonemes or the same rime 'in'). Recognizing word families and patterns helps children develop inferential self-teaching strategies. If they can read 'cake', they can work out and read 'lake' without blending all the individual phonemes.

Most teachers use both synthetic and analytic phonics, but advocates of a 'synthetics first and fast' approach claim that it is more effective in teaching children to read than mixed reading strategy approaches. They also claim that it is more effective than other kinds of phonics programmes. A recent longitudinal study in Scotland on the effectiveness of a synthetic phonics programme compared with an analytical and an analytical plus phonemic awareness programme (involving 300 children over seven years) concluded that 'the synthetic phonics approach, as part of the reading curriculum, is more effective than the analytic phonics approach' (Johnston and Watson, 2005: 9). However, a systematic review of the research literature on the use of phonics in the teaching of reading and spelling (Torgerson et al., 2006) found that the weight of evidence was weak on whether synthetic approaches were more effective than analytical approaches. They found only three randomized controlled trials on this matter (including an earlier and much smaller Scottish study of just 30 children but not including the large longitudinal Scottish study mentioned above – the experimental design used for this study did not satisfy the criteria for inclusion). They concluded that in these, no statistically significant difference in effectiveness was found between synthetic phonics instruction and analytic phonics instruction. This review confirmed the findings of Stahl et al. (1988), who also reviewed the research on phonics instruction and concluded that there are several types of good phonics instruction and that there is no research base to support the superiority of one particular type. While the Torgerson review has itself come under attack from supporters of a synthetic phonics approach (McGuinness, 2006), for the disinterested observer it would seem that currently there is not enough evidence to support the comparative claims made for synthetic versus analytic phonics. Nevertheless, the Rose Review took a pragmatic view, deciding that:

> schools and settings cannot always wait for the results of long term research studies. They must take decisions based on as much firm evidence as is available. (DfES, 2006: para. 31)

Policy decisions in England to promote synthetic phonics are not therefore based on research evidence.

Phonics as part of a wider literacy programme

The Torgerson review did, however, confirm that '*systematic* phonics instruction within a *broad* literacy curriculum was found to have a *statistically significant positive effect* on reading accuracy' (2006: 9, our italics). The Australian Reading Review and the National Reading Panel in America came to the same conclusion. These findings illuminate another area of debate – whether phonics should be a 'fast and first and only' strategy or part of a broader programme.

Some advocates of synthetic phonics programmes believe that beginning readers should only encounter phonemically decodable text in order to practise their reading skills and that there should be no 'guessing' words from picture, context or initial letter cues (see, for example, Reading Reform Foundation, 2006). They argue that using a range of cues has the potential to confuse children and that encouraging children to use information from a picture may lead to them not understanding that they must focus on the printed word (see the Rose Review, DfES, 2006: para. 117). Such a view sees reading as being a stepped process of acquiring separate reading skills. Hall (Chapter 1, this book) discusses different views of the reading process and the impact this has on people's views on phonics teaching. John Stannard's response to Rose piece in Chapter 10 looks at the model of early reading suggested in the Appendix of the Rose Review, and argues for the value of a multi-cueing system approach to reading with phonics as one (important) cue among several. Advocates of a mixed strategy approach argue that using pictures, context and syntax cues is not encouraging children to 'guess' but rather to use language knowledge, logical deduction and prior/world knowledge to make sense of a word/sentence. They would also argue that a broad literacy curriculum includes reading and being read to from a wide range of books, not just decodable texts. The Rose Review, along with the Australia and US reviews, emphasizes the importance of this.

Systematic phonics: structure and pace

Structure

Studies have been done comparing systematic phonics instruction with 'hit or miss' phonic instruction and these show that 'any kind of well organized and efficient phonics instruction is better than little or no phonic instruction that leaves phonics to chance' (Cunningham and Cunningham, 2002: 91). Systematic phonic programmes introduce phonemes in a series of steps. These usually begin with learning letter sounds, distinguishing between vowels and consonants, recognizing initial and final phonemes in regular consonant–vowel–consonant (CVC) words and introducing medial vowels. From this, simple CVC and CCVC words can be segmented and blended. Long vowels are then introduced. Different programmes may introduce consonant and vowel phonemes in different ways, but the 40-plus phonemes are introduced systematically. Farmer, Ellis and Smith's chapter on 'Teaching Phonics: The Basics' discusses the knowledge and the practical issues that need consideration when teaching a systematic phonics programme.

Although the heart of a phonics programme is the systematic introduction of phonemes in a planned sequence, teachers also use the many planned (and unplanned) opportunities to teach and apply phonic lessons that occur throughout a broad literacy curriculum. In Chapter 4, 'Inside the Classroom', Prue Goodwin and Margaret Perkins describe how, far from being 'hit and miss', a planned approach based on play and reading 'real books' can offer the opportunity to build complex phonic knowledge. We must also consider that, no matter how systematic the programme, there are many words in the English language that are just not decodable. Henrietta Dombey's chapter on English orthography (Chapter 8) helps us to see the strengths and limits of a systematic phonics programme.

Pace and when to start

If one accepts that systematic phonics teaching is necessary to beginning reader, there are strong arguments for a quick-paced programme which ensures that children have the knowledge they need to decode texts as rapidly as possible (Stahl, 1992; Wyse, 2000). The caricature of the young child plodding through an initial sound a week so that it takes almost a school year to learn 26 letter sounds is now seen as unnecessarily slow, and it is recognized that phonic programmes can be undertaken in weeks rather than months by many children. Such slowly paced practices also make the assumption that children enter school with little in the way of phonemic awareness and letter knowledge. Children begin to learn about language from the moment they are born, and both Jackie Marsh's chapter on 'Involving Parents and Carers' (Chapter 5) and Elspeth McCartney's chapter on 'Developmental Issues' (Chapter 6) remind us of the wealth of knowledge children acquire before they begin formal education. Skilled early years' practioners build on and extend children's pre-school language and speaking and listening experiences. They do not confuse a systematic approach with a formal approach. In the best early years setting, phonics is taught through active, multi-sensory strategies (language games, music and so on) embedded in a rich literacy curriculum (see, for example, Palmer and Bayley, 2004). Such phonics teaching may often be in small group contexts to allow for different developmental needs. In Chapter 4, 'Inside the Classroom', teachers Lyndsay Macnair, who uses a synthetic phonics approach, and Sally Evans, who uses a mixed synthetic and analytic approach, both show the importance of active, multi-sensory approaches in their phonics teaching.

Phonics and spelling

One of the interesting aspects about the phonics debate is how dominated it is by discussion of the relationship between phonics and reading and, consequently, how little attention is paid to the relationship between phonemic knowledge and writing. Elspeth McCartney addresses this issue (Chapter 6) when she argues that spelling errors commonly assumed to be the child making visual confusions may actually reflect errors of phonemic perception. She urges teachers to consider this possibility when looking at children's work because, clearly, the two errors need different types of support. In Chapter 7, Laura Huxford explores this further by describing the strong relationship between young writers' developmental spellings and the phonics curriculum. Her examples show how phonics within a broad and coherent literacy programme can empower children as writers. Henrietta Dombey, in Chapter 8, strikes a cautionary note, however, pointing to evidence that challenges the wisdom of total reliance on phonics. She reminds us that the opaque orthography of English means that teachers must be able to explain how the spelling of word families is deeply connected to their shared history; understanding the basis of visual and morphological patterns may be more powerful in the long term.

What next?

The 'phonics debate' has played differently in different educational systems. In Scotland, where the literacy curriculum is less centrally controlled, phonics has not become so politically charged as it has in England, Australia and the United States. Phonics research has been publicized by the Scottish Office, but decisions about how to respond to it have been left in the hands of local authorities, schools and teachers. In England the response has been different. The House of Commons Select Committee on Education set up the Rose Review to consider 'What best practice should be expected in the teaching of early reading and synthetic phonics' (DfES, 2005a: 1) in part to inform the revision of the NLS framework as well as to give clear advice on what schools should do about the teaching of phonics.

In its final report, the Review has concluded that 'synthetic phonics offers the vast majority of young children the best and most direct route to becoming skilled readers and writers' (DfES, 2006: 4) and has made a strong recommendation for further phonic training for teachers, teaching assistants and student teachers. At the same time, the NLS has been piloting an early reading programme, with increased phonics teaching in the foundation stage, to be offered to all schools. In England teachers are being given a very strong steer on how to teach phonics.

So where does this debate leave teachers who are wondering whether to alter their approach to teaching phonics in the light of new ideas and new recommendations? As a professional you will want to make a considered decision on this. Rather than focus on the technical differences between competing programmes, you may find it more helpful to consider the principles of good phonics teaching and how these apply to your existing practice. You will weigh the evidence, look at existing practice and its outcomes as well as new ideas and their possible outcomes; you will consider your own knowledge and understanding and think of the context of your school and the needs of your pupils. You will want to discuss phonics practice with colleagues in your school and if possible from a wider network of schools. At the end of each chapter in this book are suggestions to help you consider what you are already doing and what else you might do. Chapter 11 suggests how you might use this book to initiate and support professional dialogue about phonics. There is also a Glossary which explains any technical vocabulary that might be unfamiliar to you.

There is an old story about a man who goes to his lawyer with a legal problem. The lawyer agrees his fee with the client and then reaches for a book. He opens it and reads out the answer to the man's question. The man is furious. 'It's disgraceful: I've just paid you a fortune to read a paragraph from a book. How can you possibly justify that?' 'You've got it wrong,' said the lawyer. 'I wasn't paid to read the paragraph. What you paid for was my knowledge about which paragraph, and which book. The reading was free.'

Like that lawyer, teachers are not paid just for 'doing' a set curriculum; they are paid to make professional decisions about the needs of the children they teach, and for the knowledge that underpins these decisions. We hope the contributions in this book will add to that store of professional knowledge and enable teachers to make wise decisions.

Chapter 1

How Children Learn to Read and How Phonics Helps

Kathy Hall

Underachievement in education is a perennial hot topic in the public view and children's reading achievement is at the centre of this conversation. This is despite the fact that the most recent evidence would suggest that the teaching of reading is successful for the vast majority of children in England with 87 per cent of girls and 82 per cent of boys achieving level 4 or above in the 2005 Key Stage 2 tests (DfES, 2005b). But a substantial minority of children do not achieve well, constituting the so-called 'long tail of underachievement' that has become characteristic of education in this country and that attests to many children not reaching their potential. To improve reading achievement overall there is still plenty of work to be done by educators, policymakers, researchers, media people and publishers.

My focus in this chapter is on the teacher and the school. I will begin by considering key factors that influence how children learn to read and then I will attend more specifically to word recognition and the role of phonics. A message deriving from my argument is that it is unwise to advance an exclusive method of teaching the alphabetic principle. I will argue that such a prescriptive stance denies the complexity of teaching and learning and that the marginalization or exclusion of other methods ignores the psychological and linguistic evidence about phonological and phonemic sensitivity in beginning readers. The chapter suggests a better way forward.

Learning, teaching and the whole of reading

A major reason why controversy exists about how best to develop reading (or indeed any area of the curriculum) is that fundamental differences exist in our views about knowledge and how we come to know. If one sees knowledge as fixed and certain and 'out there', separate from the knower, literacy can be viewed as an individual and linear accomplishment, made up of a discrete set of skills like phonics, fluency and comprehension. If one takes this perspective one is more likely to see teaching as a prescriptive business in which curriculum content is presented, unmediated by context or the nature of learning relationships, in small increments to the learner. In addition, one is more likely to accept the possibility of there being just one best way to help all pupils learn to read.

If, on the other hand, one sees knowledge (including knowledge about the alphabet) as something that is actively built up and appropriated by learners' active participation in tasks, if one sees learners as intentional beings whose wider knowledge, feelings, experiences and identities constantly filter their understanding, if one considers that what learners see as significant in a task or particular learning situation influences what they can take away from it in terms of new learning, then one is more likely to see teaching as a process which must engage with the learner's take on the world, especially the learner's view of themselves and the learning context. Here teaching, learning and knowledge are viewed as intimately related. In this perspective, literacy involves more than merely an interest in whether children can read and write; it involves questions about what learners do with their literacy, the literacy practices that are meaningful to them and the literacy practices they engage in in their day-to-day lives. If one goes along with this line of thinking, one is less likely to accept directives about there being one best way of helping pupils to read. These fundamental beliefs and assumptions are often ignored in discussions about the best way to teach reading, and they very often underlie controversies about teaching methods.

To teach children to read involves more than helping them know about letters and sounds. Teaching children to understand the alphabetic principle is important for successful reading, but it's only one of the many factors which need be considered. The elements of reading that teachers have to consider as they plan curricula, programmes and teaching strategies are shown in Figure 1.1. To concentrate in our teaching (or indeed in our policy making) on only one of those aspects is to ignore the larger system, any element or combination of elements of which can produce failure. Such a narrow view gives the false impression that the way to enhance the teaching of reading is simple and straightforward – that all it needs is one solution involving one method or one programme.

As the US researchers who produced this diagram point out, any single aspect needs to be seen in the context of a literacy curriculum that considers all aspects. This means that learning the alphabetic principle cannot be divorced from the notion of ownership or engagement or motivation to read. Desire to read is necessary for the sustained effort needed to become a proficient reader and teachers cannot afford to ignore this, especially as recent evidence points to the disparity between the incidence of children in this country and in other European countries who read for pleasure and enjoyment (Mullis et al., 2003).

The development of the alphabetic principle cannot be separated from comprehension or writing. After all, the purpose of teaching the alphabetic

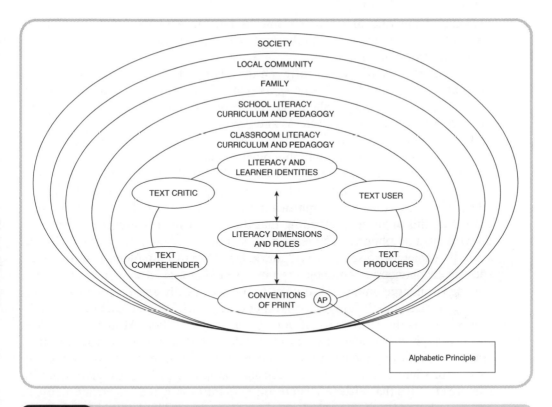

Figure 1.1 Dimensions of literacy (adapted from Taylor et al., 2000: 18)

principle is to facilitate comprehension. Because reading involves different kinds of literature, children need to learn to read different kinds of texts and a school may promote or neglect this with consequences for reading achievement. We also have to consider the fit between home and school literacies. As Taylor et al. (2000) point out, children's home languages may be built upon, marginalized or totally ignored by the school. Children may have family literacy experiences that fit well with the expectations of the school or those experiences may go unrecognized, all with consequences for pupils' opportunities to learn and for their life chances. Similar arguments can be made for the importance of the other aspects in the diagram because all of them influence reading achievement. The fact is that any literacy curriculum exists within a broader social context that can enhance or militate against ability to read and write.

Understanding the phonics debate

A major reading theme currently exercising educators, policymakers, researchers, media people and publishers in the United Kingdom concerns the beginning reader and the role of phonics. How best to develop the necessary phonic knowledge in the classroom and whether current policy has got it right are deeply controversial questions.

In essence this controversy centres on the relative effectiveness of two different methods of teaching phonics, known as synthetic and analytic phonics. Crudely put, synthetic phonics is about sounding out and blending, while analytic phonics is about perceiving patterns and drawing inferences (definitions of these and other terms are provided in the Glossary). In addition, synthetic phonics has come to be associated with small phonological units (phonemes) linked to letters, and analytic phonics has come to be associated with large phonological units (onsets and rimes) also linked to letters and letter strings (for example, White, 2005). However, at least one significant researcher in the field (Goswami, 2002: 52) rejects this alignment, claiming that the onset–rime research has nothing to do with analytic phonics. The alignment stems, in my view, from the claims in some psychological research that knowledge of small phonological units, more specifically phonemic knowledge, is a better predictor of success in reading than knowledge of large phonological units (more specifically onsets and rimes). This finding has led, unhelpfully, to a corresponding polarization of teaching methods.

Research at the University of York (Hulme et al., 2002; Muter et al., 2004) shows that phonemic awareness is an excellent predictor of early reading skills, and those researchers have argued that measures of onset–rime awareness are weaker predictors. This work also claims that explicit phoneme-level training is more effective than rhyme-level training in improving reading attainments in children deemed to be at risk of reading difficulties. The Scottish research in Clackmannanshire (Johnston and Watson, 2005), which was set up to assess the relative merits of synthetic and analytic teaching approaches, highlights the value of explicit phoneme-level training linked to letters. Other research too makes similar claims about the relative effectiveness of synthetic phonics over analytic phonics (e.g. Stuart, 1999; Macmillan, 2002; Chew, 1997). So it would seem that an emphasis on small phonological units, specifically phonemes, is important and this is in line with an emphasis on synthetic phonics.

Much of this research has been criticized on the grounds that it is asking the wrong research question, since both large and small phonological units are necessary for reading. The Scottish research, which has had considerable exposure especially in the popular press, can be severely criticized on the basis of a flawed design leading to claims about the effectiveness of synthetic phonics that are unjustified by the evidence. I would suggest that analytic phonics was set up for failure in the Scottish study, while synthetic phonics was set up for success. This in no way disputes the need for phonemic knowledge, but it does highlight the origin of the needless oppositional positioning that has developed in the debate surrounding research, policy and practice.

In my view the evidence converges on the conclusion that attention to small *and* large units in early reading instruction is helpful for all children. Insofar as synthetic and analytic phonics are associated respectively with small and large units, then both teaching approaches are likely to be useful and complementary. The next sections develop this argument further.

Clues about a developmental sequence and progression

It is likely that some children would fail to benefit from approaches designed to teach phoneme sensitivity linked to letters (that is, synthetic phonics) if they do not possess the necessary phonological knowledge. The latter could be developed through oral language, songs, rhymes, riddles, word play in stories, and invented spelling. 'I spy', rhyming stories, nursery rhymes, tongue twisters and poems all have an important part to play, as well as games, activities and exercises. Exposure to intensive programmes aimed at teaching explicit phoneme manipulation may only serve to discourage children who have not grasped the phonological insight that spoken language can be broken up into units like syllables and onsets and rime.

One researcher (Stahl, 1992) explains this well with reference to the case of a girl, Heather, whose lack of progress and apparent incapacity to benefit from phonics in class were of concern. He sought to gain a sense of her level of phonological awareness by asking her questions like the following: Can you say the word 'meat' without the /m/sound? ('eat'), Can you say the word 'coat' without the /k/sound? ('oat'). Heather's answers to these two questions respectively were 'chicken' and 'jacket'. Puzzled about this, he pursued his line of questioning to discover that she had not understood that spoken language can be thought about without reference to its meaning. As far as Heather was concerned, a little bit of 'meat' was 'chicken' and a little bit of 'coat' was 'jacket' – she was responding to language at the level of meaning, not at the abstract level required for the manipulation of sounds in one's head. Until Heather grasped this insight, a strong focus on phonemic awareness would probably be unhelpful to her. This raises what is one of the hallmarks of good reading teaching – understanding your learners, recognizing what is salient for them in the moment-by-moment interaction in a lesson, as well as having a sense of how best to sequence the curriculum to maximize their learning.

There is good evidence that the development of phonological skills proceeds from early awareness of large units (syllables, onset–rimes) to later awareness of small units (phonemes) (Bowey, 2002). But there is a subtle distinction to be noted here which derives from the research of Usha Goswami (2002). This shows that while onsets and rimes are the most accessible phonological units, letters are the most salient orthographic units for the beginning reader. Her work tells us that it is easier for children to learn the phonemes which are onsets (initial phonemes) or rimes. This line of work suggests an important message about progression: it may be helpful to teach the phonemes that are onsets and rimes first, and then move on to other phonemes.

However, having made the point about a possible developmental sequence, I would suggest that teachers need not be entirely bound by this. The fact is that learning is not only a cognitive process, it is also a social and cultural one as I noted earlier in the chapter. Individual cognition is always embedded within a particular social context (Razfar and Gutierrez, 2003). While the psychological evidence offers clues about how we might teach the alphabetic principle, it cannot determine it for us for the same reasons I have raised about the nature of learning and knowledge. Children, like all people, learn concepts and practices, including phonological and phonemic knowledge, not as simple linear content; rather, learning occurs unevenly and flexibly and by having many varied opportunities for interaction, for practice, for application and reflection on its purposes and processes. We should not be dogmatic about the fine details of curriculum content any more than we should be dogmatic about the details of teaching methods.

The human brain and pattern recognition

The brain is an exquisitely designed pattern detector (Bussis et al., 1985), so it makes sense to capitalize on this talent. As the reader sees patterns repeatedly (such as *ai* in *mail*, *paint* and *constrain*), the graphic letter pattern is retained in memory in association with sound. When a familiar pattern is detected in a word, that pattern evokes those stored associations. This then enables the reader to decode a new word like *complaint* (see Johnston, 2001 for a full account; also Ehri, 2005). Word sorting activities, usually a key feature of analytic phonics, encourage learners to notice patterns, to think flexibly about letter–sound correspondences. Such activities support self-teaching, whereby the learner develops a means of identifying the sound of unknown words independently. Once this self-teaching mechanism is under way the reader can begin to use larger visual sequences that map onto larger phonological units. In this way reading becomes indistinguishable from whole-word reading.

The issue of generalizability and pattern detection begs an important question: how much phonemic knowledge does the teacher need to teach? By virtue of the human brain's pattern detection abilities, a teacher may not need to work through all of the 40-plus phonemes of English. Understanding that the initial sounds of the written words 'mat' and 'mop' are the same (that is, mastery of the singleton onset), coupled with relevant letter–sound knowledge, may be sufficient for the alphabetic principle to be grasped by some children (Bowey, 2002; Byrne, 2005). Some children helped to recognize the identity of word beginnings are readily able to transfer their insight to word endings; others cannot transfer automatically and quickly – they need more help and practice.

All of this complicates the process for the teacher and certainly suggests that it's not sensible to prescribe one programme or method that all children should experience. Even if one adopts a narrow cognitive perspective on learning, the fact is that there cannot be any single theory of how children should be taught to read as children have different capacities to generalize (Byrne, 2005).

Causes and consequences of phonemic sensitivity

Some interpretations of synthetic phonics emphasize that learners should be taught the sound of letters and common letter blends before they move on to reading books. But if one accepts, which inevitably one must, that phoneme awareness is both a cause and a consequence of letter knowledge or learning to recognize printed words, then this position is untenable. And if one accepts that many children come to school already seeing themselves as readers (and writers), it makes no sense to delay their reading of books, not to mention the potential damage of communicating to them that they can't read. Notwithstanding the status attributed to synthetic phonics in their work, the York researchers conclude that there is a reciprocal relationship between phoneme sensitivity and reading achievement. For example, Hulme et al. say that 'a reasonable conclusion is that in the literate individual there is a constant interaction between phonological and orthographic representations' (2005: 97). They draw this conclusion from their finding that letter knowledge at 4 years 9 months is a predictor of phoneme sensitivity one year later and, conversely, phoneme sensitivity at 4 years 9 months is a predictor of letter knowledge one year later (Muter et al., 2004). Other researchers, too, reported a similar reciprocal pattern (Lupker, 2005). The point here is that as the child reads more and generally appropriates more linguistic knowledge of reading, vocabulary and spelling, phonemic knowledge also increases.

So phonological knowledge, phonemic knowledge and letter name knowledge are interconnected. This is concretely described in *The Learning Brain* by Blakemore and Frith as follows: 'Think of two groups of children each playing with a toy village. One group has ready-made wooden houses while the other has houses constructed out of Lego bricks. Those who have the Lego brick houses will consider the town as infinitely modifiable, whereas the children with the wooden houses will think of their houses as fixed and whole. For them, the concept of being able to remove pieces from each house and change the shape of the houses makes no sense' (2005: 73). The thing is that once learners grasp the alphabetic principle, their whole view of speech changes, for they are now aware that the sounds of words can be broken up and put back together again. In addition, they now have a technique for making up words that do not exist. Prior to acquiring this insight, made-up words are only thought of as 'existing, but unknown, words' (2005: 73).

In relation to phonological awareness, what appears to happen is that knowledge which was, up until the acquisition of the alphabetic principle, deeply embedded and implicit now becomes foregrounded and explicit. The teacher's job, then, is to help children make explicit the phonological knowledge that they already possess about onsets and rimes. They need to be helped to segment onsets and rimes even further when these units correspond to groups of phonemes (Goswami, 2002).

The complex orthography of English

The alphabet is the visual code for representing oral language. Learning how to crack this code would be much simpler if there was just one letter for every sound (or phoneme). But there are almost twice as many phonemes as letters, and each letter is used to represent several sounds in different contexts – note for instance the 't' in 'nation', 'native' and 'nature'. English has a 'deep' orthography unlike say Finnish, German or Greek. (Henrietta Dombey explores the impact of deep orthography on learning to read and spell in Chapter 8.) The point is that the relative inconsistency in mappings of letters and sounds makes learning to read English much harder than learning to read many other languages (Goswami, 2005; Ziegler and Goswami, 2005). Some words in English, for example 'people', 'yacht' and 'choir', represent no pattern in the language in that there are no other words with similar sound-letter mappings or, put more technically, they have no 'orthographic neighbours' (Zeigler and Goswami, 2005: 19) and must be learned as distinct patterns. A whole word approach therefore is relevant for such words. Once again this highlights the inadequacy of using just one teaching method.

Spotlight on comprehension

Comprehension is of course the purpose of decoding, and word recognition is merely the means to this. Successful comprehension depends on skills beyond the phonological domain. The York research has shown that vocabulary knowledge and grammar knowledge predict reading comprehension, even when the effects of word recognition, phoneme sensitivity and letter knowledge are controlled (Muter et al., 2004). That reading comprehension is heavily dependent on semantic and syntactic language skills is obvious to anyone who has ever supported a child's understanding of printed text. However, the nature of vocabulary and comprehension bears some comparative scrutiny with alphabetic knowledge.

Letter and phonic knowledge is finite. All of it (names of letters and the correspondences between phonemes and graphemes) is usually learned quickly and everyone learns the same knowledge. All readers go from non-existent knowledge of the alphabetic principle through full acquisition to automatic word recognition. This knowledge, though absolutely vital, also has a narrow sphere of impact – it impacts on decoding only. On the other hand, vocabulary and comprehension knowledge develop over the life span, are probably infinite in range and vocabulary and comprehension competence can vary enormously between individuals. In a seminal research paper published recently in the United States, Scott Paris (2005) explains this idea and suggests a crucial distinction between what he terms 'constrained' and 'unconstrained' reading skills. Constrained skills have 'a narrow scope, are learned quickly, the trajectory of mastery is steep and the duration of acquisition is brief' (Paris, 2005: 188). Constrained skills are likely to have a limited range of influence on reading achievement beyond the early stages. Unconstrained reading skills like vocabulary and comprehension are a different matter, he suggests. These develop over one's entire life and show enduring differences across individuals. And very importantly from the perspective of the current policy context, these skills develop before, during and after constrained skills like word recognition.

This notion of constraincd and unconstrained reading skills has enormous implications for the theory of reading and the statistical methods used to predict reading achievement. Space prevents a full account of Paris' analysis here, but suffice to say it casts serious doubt on some of the existing reading research that claims privileged status for word recognition skill over comprehension and on the research that claims privileged status for any one way of developing this knowledge. While Paris notes how important it is that the beginning reader masters constrained aspects, his analysis leads him to the conclusion that any single pedagogical approach should not be privileged over any other. He expresses this as follows: 'What is unscientific, illogical, and unwarranted are the claims that one kind of instruction is the best or only way to promote the acquisition of the skills, that those methods are uniformly appropriate for all children, that the constrained skills have greater priority over other skills, and that such interventions prevent reading failure' (Paris, 2005: 199).

So what is a teacher to do? The skill of word recognition is crucial for successful reading and the first couple of years in school are especially significant for its mastery. But since word recognition is probably not the only mediator of reading comprehension (Paris, 2005) – and reading comprehension is the purpose of word recognition – other, unconstrained, skills need to be developed in tandem.

To sum up so far, reading requires the integration of information from at least six different areas of knowledge:

- *Cultural*: learners bring with them knowledge and beliefs about the reading activities they are engaged in; they have views about themselves as particular people in relation with other people, for example, how they wish to be recognized by their peer group; in sum they have identities and are active agents in the learning enterprise.
- *Communicative*: concepts about print, about genres, since different texts have different intentions and purposes.
- *Verbal reasoning*: literal and inferential reasoning ability and the ability to understand, for example, metaphor.
- *Phonic knowledge:* visual and aural perception of letters and phoneme–grapheme relations.
- *Semantic:* meaning of the words.
- *Syntactic:* grammar of sentences and larger units.

Since these are interdependent and support each other it makes sense for the teacher to be mindful of all of them. This of course need not preclude selecting an element such as phonic knowledge for particular attention within lessons, but the accomplished teacher considers all these processes, as the next section explains.

What do we know about what accomplished teachers do in reading lessons?

Classroom research generally shows that teachers make a larger difference in learners' growth as readers than do the methods those teachers are nominally using (Taylor and Pearson, 2002). Research on effective literacy teaching shows conclusively that a quality literacy programme is not merely about teaching materials, the curriculum and set procedures. The most critical element in building an effective reading programme is the teacher (Hall, 2003). Also, accomplished teachers make more impact in schools located in high poverty areas than they do in schools in economically advantaged areas. This is not surprising when one considers how children who are poorer depend more on their school and their teachers to socialize them into school literacy practices. This suggests that providing teacher professional development would be the most reliable way to improve reading attainment.

In addition, as well as strong teacher effects, there are strong school effects on pupil success in reading. This suggests the importance of professional development for all school staff members, including support staff and teaching assistants, and not simply classroom teachers. A major US government-commissioned study of effective reading teaching is especially revealing here. It took account also of organizational factors at the school and district levels and concluded that 'effective instruction includes artful teaching that transcends – and often makes up for – the constraints and limitations of specific instructional programs' (Snow et al., 1998: 314). What all this tells us is that simply prescribing an evidence-based method to teaching reading (that's if we knew of such a single one) is far from enough – how such an approach is implemented by teachers in the classroom is critical.

The pedagogic practices of the most accomplished teachers are noteworthy. They are subtle, flexible, personalized, learner-focused and context-aware. They include:

- *Integration and application*: The notion of integration captures this idea and is better than 'balance' in conveying what accomplished teachers do. Integration is more sophisticated than mixing a little bit of this and a little bit of that. It involves teaching word recognition or how to crack the code alongside the development of comprehension. While they offer systematic teaching in language conventions to foster letter–sound correspondences, accomplished teachers understand that the application of this knowledge to print is key: first, children need to see the rewards to be gained from the effort expended, second, learners need extensive experience of applying phonic knowledge to running text, and third, they need instruction and support in making sense of text (UKLA, 2005).

- *Coaching*: Accomplished teachers coach weak readers often in one-to-one and small group settings. In a study of successful one-on-one tutoring of struggling early readers, practitioners used a range of methods to make children's implicit knowledge explicit, including:

  - reading texts that provided multiple repetitions of the same words and word families;
  - providing direct teaching about the letter–sound relations within words;
  - helping children to spell words through numerous teacher-scaffolded interactions; and
  - hearing the teacher's words as the teacher models how to identify or spell unknown words.

  All these activities are personalized, which means they are delivered at the right moment and repeated as frequently as needed for an individual child to understand, internalize and recall (Juel and Minden-Cupp, 2001).

- *Instructional density*: Accomplished teachers are adept at fostering several aspects of learning in one short teaching episode; they are able to seize teaching opportunities as they arise and link them with their planned teaching.

- *Extensive experiences with an array of texts*: Accomplished teachers draw on a broad curriculum using meaningful and varied texts for purposes that mirror reading and writing in the real world. Authenticity characterizes their approach in that the reading activities they facilitate are closely linked with reading in everyday life outside of school.

- *Formative assessment*: Accomplished teachers have a style of teaching that is more conversational than interrogational; they tune in to what their learners say and do with a view to understanding their interpretations and misconceptions so that they can intervene appropriately. They build on their learners' responses, seeing what their learners say as evidence of their thinking and understanding. In this way they are seeking to understand what is salient to the learner.

- *Grouping*: Children are grouped and regrouped for teaching purposes rather than fixed ability groups; small group teaching, one-to-one teaching and whole class teaching are judiciously blended. Whole class phonics teaching is not likely to be effective for the majority of children. The key to reaching a child by providing verbal interactions, instruction and written materials that are at the right level and at the right time is simply not as easy in the whole class setting.

To summarize, the classroom practices of accomplished reading teachers make it clear that they see their learners as intentional beings and that they see learning itself as a volitional process. They also see themselves as powerful enablers who are aware of the connection between what they do in the classroom and their learners' success as readers. They are adept at adapting learning environments to suit their particular learners. Accomplished teachers seem to have a strong sense of what is personally meaningful to their learners and have the capacity to exploit and explore this in their interactions with learners. Their practices are evidence-informed about learners as well as about literacy learning.

Why won't programmes work?

The idea of solving reading difficulties via the curriculum or via a teaching method is seductive, but there are many reasons why schemes, programmes or curricula are an inadequate basis for improving practice. How the schemes, programmes or the curricula get translated into learning can't be predetermined – as already noted, teaching and learning have to be considered in tandem. The problem with mandating schemes and programmes is that they cannot take into account the contexts of their implementation and thus they cannot place the learner at the centre of the learning enterprise.

Also, from the perspective of teachers and teaching, the more we dictate teachers' moves and script their lines, the more we're likely to alienate good teachers. In the United States, heavily scripted phonics lessons and programmes are routinely marketed as compensation for poor teachers. What's not mentioned is that they also alienate and even drive out good teachers. It is imperative that such a situation should not develop here.

Phonics is 'big business', with financial rewards awaiting anyone who invents 'the best' scheme or programme for teaching it. In the United States there are various 'lobbies' whose existence and lobbying have the potential to distort the 'normal research' investigations and national and local policy processes. Such lobbying can be counter-productive for pupils; it stimulates practice, policy and research in artificially narrow domains without encouraging consideration of the broader picture outlined in the early part of this chapter. In addition, lobbies almost always distort policy and research by introducing a political and an adversarial dimension where polarities and simplifications win out over the realities and complexities. Six years ago Colin Harrison (1999) observed that whenever you get a situation where there isn't agreement among members of the research community, as we currently have about the teaching of phonics, rhetoric and lobbying often become the basis on which decisions about teaching come to be made. While this lack of consensus remains, it is my view that the theory of reading pedagogy has progressed, especially through the work of significant researchers like Usha Goswami (see especially, for example, Zeigler and Goswami, 2005), and this line of work has clearer implications for practice than were available six years ago. On the basis of the review of evidence conducted by the USA's National Reading Panel (NRP) (2000b), we also know that the teaching of phonics is essential for the beginning reader and that phonics is best developed in a systematic way. The NRP review also showed how *several* methods of teaching phonics in the classroom are successful, but found that the methods themselves were significantly indistinguishable in their effects. This was also the conclusion reached in a more recent systematic review of evidence (Torgerson et al., 2006).

Conclusion

Phonics teaching is far from all that beginning readers need to became successful readers. They need to have experience of a wide range of literature – fiction and non-fiction – so that they learn about the pleasure and knowledge that can come from being read to and from reading for oneself. Beginning readers must be taught how to use all the cues and strategies that will help them make sense of text and this will include strategies to decode words as well as strategies for comprehending text. Phonics teaching is an important part of this story, but it is not the whole story.

SOMETHING TO THINK ABOUT

- In what ways are teacher beliefs about teaching and learning important?
- How do your beliefs about phonics and the teaching of phonics influence what you do in the classroom?
- If you were trying to understand the teaching of phonics in your school, how would this chapter help you to go about doing this?

SOMETHING TO READ

- Goswami, U. (2005) 'Synthetic phonics and learning to read: A cross language perspective', *Educational Psychology in Practice*, 21 (4): 273–82.

- Cook, M. (ed.) (2002) *Perspectives on the Teaching and Learning of Phonics*. Royston: United Kingdom Literacy Association.

- Hall, K. (2003b) *Listening to Stephen Read: Multiple Perspectives on Literacy*. Buckingham: Open University Press. pp. 67–101.

SOMETHING TO DO

- Talk with a colleague about why the phonics debate is so heated. You might locate a suitable article in the popular press to focus your talk.
- Examine one of the phonics schemes and consider the assumptions it makes about how best to develop children's acquisition of the alphabetic principle. Is it in line with a) your views and b) the evidence presented in this chapter?
- Revisit Figure 1.1 and talk with a colleague about 'the place of phonics' and 'putting phonics in its place'.

Chapter 2

Learning to Read the Words on the Page: The Crucial Role of Early Phonics Teaching

Morag Stuart

Reading is one of the most miraculous of human achievements. Learning to read is one of the most important acts of learning required of children. Small wonder, then, that how children can best be taught to read has been fiercely debated down through the ages. Reading is also complex, and the word itself is subject to many different definitions and interpretations. We read in order to understand written language – language we see – just as we listen in order to understand spoken language – language we hear. For understanding to happen in reading, we need to process visually presented information (written words). For understanding to happen in listening, we need to process aurally presented information (spoken words). One of the major differences between reading and listening is thus the nature of the information to be processed: the written versus the spoken word. Human beings are biologically endowed to process the spoken word; processing the written word, however, is a culturally determined skill that has to be taught and learned.

This chapter is intended as an introduction to research into the ways in which human beings learn to process the written word: research that seeks to understand how children come to be able to look at any visually presented word, whether it is presented in a context or by itself, and read it aloud and understand what it means. Unless children do develop efficient processes for recognizing written words, they will not be able to understand written texts; but development of efficient word recognition and comprehension processes does not guarantee understanding at the textual level. Reading the words is a necessary but not a sufficient condition for the understanding of written texts to take place. This chapter, then, investigates only the necessary condition – the ability to read the words on the page.

A child's route to reading

Let's take an imaginary child – always easier to deal with than a real one! Chelsea is five, and she's just starting school. We are going to follow Chelsea's journey from not being able to read the words on the page, to doing this with a certain degree of ease: from pre-reader to word reader. Chelsea is going to be a child who takes to reading as naturally as a duck takes to water, and we are going to learn what it is that enables her to be so rapidly successful.

At five, Chelsea's oral vocabulary is well within the average range for her age: she is a typically developing 5-year-old in terms of her ability to understand and produce spoken words. Her grammatical system is also well within the average range for her age: she is also a typically developing 5-year-old in terms of her ability to understand and produce a range of different sentence structures. Chelsea is as well able to understand spoken messages and stories as any other typically developing 5-year-old. In her short life, she has experienced the full range of experiences that one might expect an inner-city 5-year-old like Chelsea to have experienced. She has attended morning sessions at nursery since she was three and a half. She goes to the shops with her mum, and spends time on the swings in the local playground. She is invited to birthday parties. She travels on buses and in cars, and sometimes on trains. She goes to the doctor. She also frequently visits her nan who lives nearby, and sometimes her granny who now lives by the sea. Her parents, grandparents and nursery teachers/carers have read her lots of stories. We might therefore expect, given her age-appropriate language system and her range of childhood experiences, that once Chelsea learns to read the words on the page, she will be as well able as any typically developing 5-year-old to understand the stories she reads. What essential attributes does Chelsea bring to the task of learning to read the words on the page?

Chelsea learned quite a lot about letters before she started school. She'd had an alphabet frieze in her bedroom, and her nan had a favourite alphabet book that they used to enjoy together. At nursery, she learned the alphabet song, and began to write her name. There was an alphabet frieze at nursery too, and Chelsea and her friends sometimes played at copying the letters from that. By the time she was five, Chelsea could name many of the letters on the alphabet frieze. Knowledge of letter names has frequently been identified in the research literature as a reliable predictor of success in learning to read words: this might be one of the factors that contributed to Chelsea's capacity to take to reading like a duck to water.

Alphabet books and friezes tend to illustrate each letter with an object whose name starts with the sound of that letter (a picture of a bear to go with 'b'; a picture of an egg to go with 'e' and so on). So, at five, Chelsea had also begun to realize that letters had sounds as well as names, and she'd begun to associate some of the letters with the sounds they represented. She knew that 'm' was /m/ for mummy, 'd' was /d/ for daddy, 'n' was /n/ for nan, 'b' was /b/ for bear.

From the nursery rhymes her nan taught her, and the rhyming songs and games she played at nursery, Chelsea had got the idea of rhyme. If you asked her what rhymed with 'cat', she could tell you that 'bat' did, and so did 'lat' and 'dat'. She was beginning to be able to categorize words by the sound patterns they had in common – beginning to be 'phonologically aware'. At its broadest, phonological awareness involves being able to turn away from the meanings of words and pay attention to their form. Chelsea, like many other young children, became aware first of rhymes. But by the time she started school, Chelsea could also tell you what sound a word started with: that 'cat' began with /k/ and 'dog' with /d/. She probably was helped towards this by her experience with the alphabet books and friezes, where letters were illustrated by objects whose names began with the sound of the letter, and by the day-to-day exchanges at home where /m/ was for mummy and /d/ for daddy.

Understanding the alphabetic principle

And here we come to the most crucial influence on Chelsea's flying start in learning how to read words: by the time she started school, she had already begun to understand the alphabetic principle. She knew that there were letters. She knew that letters could be named and written. She knew that spoken words were composed of sounds. She knew that those sounds could be represented by letters. There is ample research evidence that children who understand these aspects of the alphabetic principle are likely to learn to read words quickly and easily (see, for example, Bus and van Ijzendoorn, 1999; Foorman et al., 2003; Mann and Foy, 2003; Treiman, 2000). Moreover, as Brian Byrne has shown in his important longitudinal studies, providing children with *teaching* that enables them to understand the alphabetic principle before they start school has long-lasting beneficial effects on their ability to read the words on the page (1998: 75–106).

According to David Share (1995), these long-lasting beneficial effects occur because young children who understand the alphabetic principle and who are taught letter–sound rules (elementary phonics) as their first introduction to reading have a powerful self-teaching device available. They can 'sound out' and hence pronounce unfamiliar words that they come across in their reading. If the word is one that is already in their spoken vocabulary, sounding out and pronouncing it will allow them to understand it. If it is a word that is not in their spoken vocabulary, the context in which it appears will give them some idea of what it might mean, thus contributing to oral vocabulary development. Using phonic rules to sound out unfamiliar words thus has the power to develop both written and spoken vocabulary. Furthermore, Share argues that paying close attention to the letter-by-letter sequence of the unfamiliar word as it is sounded out facilitates its storage in sight vocabulary (by sight vocabulary, we mean a store of words that are instantly recognized on sight, and linked to their meanings and pronunciations).

Chelsea was lucky, in that her first teacher understood the place and value of early phonics teaching, and provided the children in her class with systematic and structured teaching of letter–sound correspondences. This wise and wonderful teacher also made sure that it was fun for the children, and that they immediately had opportunities to practise their new knowledge in reading and writing words using the letter–sound rules they'd learned, and the segmenting and blending skills they'd been taught. Chelsea was soon well placed to start trying to sound out unfamiliar words, as she had been taught letter sounds and how to blend these to make words. She had a powerful toolkit to help her decode transparent two-, three- and four-letter words like 'up', 'hat', 'went' and so on. Her self-teaching device was kicking in from the beginning. Her phoneme segmentation skills and knowledge of letter sounds also enabled her to start to write without needing continual adult input to this – her spelling was not conventional, but she was able to represent the sound pattern of most words she wanted to write (for example, 'plez wil u cum to mi prte').

Acquiring sight vocabulary

Chelsea also took part in shared reading sessions with big books. She often looked at the big book herself once the session had ended, and played school with her friend, when they took turns in being the teacher and reading the big book. Because the same big books were shared frequently in reading sessions, Chelsea very quickly learned several of the texts off by heart. Then, her 'playing school' sessions with her friend became real learning sessions: Chelsea was careful to follow each word in the text with her finger, as the teacher did, and to recite the text she had learned by heart as she did so. Most often, the word she recited was the word she was pointing to and looking at, although there were occasional mismatches – 5-year-olds are not necessarily perfect at identifying word boundaries in connected speech, so her recitation occasionally ran ahead of her pointing. When the word attended to on the page matched the word she was speaking, Chelsea had the opportunity to learn that that particular arrangement of printed letters represented that particular spoken word. She was able also to start storing some sight vocabulary.

Jackie Masterson, Maureen Dixon and I carried out a training experiment (Stuart et al., 2000) to see how easy it is for 5-year-old beginning readers to store new words in sight vocabulary from repeated shared reading of the same texts. It turned out to be much harder than we expected! We tried to teach the children 16 new words, which were printed in red to make them identifiable as the words to be learned. There was one of the red words on each page. After the children had seen and read each red word 36 times, no child was able to read all 16 of them, and the average number of words read correctly was five. We were quite shocked by this, because we had made a database of all the words from all the books the children were reading in school, and so we knew how many different words each child had been exposed to in their first term reading at school. This ranged from 39 to 277 different words, with a mean of 126. Hardly any of these words occurred frequently in any individual child's pool of vocabulary: on average fewer than four words occurred more than 20 times – yet 36 repetitions had not been enough to guarantee that children would remember a word. When we tested children's ability to read words they'd experienced more than 20 times in their school reading, on average they could read only one word correctly.

The alphabetic principle and learning sight vocabulary

Chelsea would have been one of the stars if she had taken part in our experiment. We had actually split the children into two groups, based on their knowledge of letters and their ability to give the first sound in a spoken word. One group had, like Chelsea, good understanding of the alphabetic principle. They were near perfect at telling us that 'sandwich' began with /s/, and at choosing the written letter S as the one you'd need if you were going to start writing 'sandwich'. We'll call this group the 'graphophonic group'. The other group had no idea what 'sandwich' or any other spoken word we presented started with, and made random choices when asked which letter you'd need if you were going to start writing 'sandwich' or any other word we'd presented. We'll call this group the 'non-graphophonic group'. The graphophonic group learned significantly more of the new words than the non-graphophonic group: after 36 encounters with each word, the graphophonic group could on average read seven words and the non-graphophonic group only three.

We suggested that two things – awareness of phonemes in spoken words, and letter–sound knowledge – are crucial to this swifter acquisition of sight vocabulary. Sight vocabulary involves forming links between the visual form of the word and its meaning and pronunciation. The link from the visual form of a word to its meaning is essentially arbitrary. If, like Chelsea, and like the children in the graphophonic group, you can also make some logical links between some of the letters in the visual form of the word and some of the sounds you can hear in the spoken word, this should underpin and reinforce the arbitrary link from visual form to meaning. This, we suggest, is why the graphophonic group who could identify initial sounds in words and map from a sound to a letter learned more words than the non-graphophonic group. Similar suggestions have been made by Linnea Ehri (1995) and Usha Goswami (1993).

Interestingly, we had also measured the children's visual memory abilities, because making links between visual forms of words and their meanings could be seen as involving visual memory – memory for things you have seen. Our two groups of children were matched for visual memory ability. For children in the graphophonic group, there was no correlation between visual memory scores and number of words learned. But for children in the non-graphophonic group, this correlation was highly significant: although children in this group learned fewer words, the children with better visual memory scores were more likely to learn some words. It seems that if a child has no understanding or knowledge of the alphabetic principle, then they'd better have a good visual memory.

The fact that we'd found evidence not only of differential rates of learning but also that the two groups were perhaps trying to set up representations of words based on entirely different kinds of information led us to a further question, namely, what aspects of printed words do children store in their earliest representations of sight vocabulary? Some children seem to be able to use logical links between print and sound to remember sight vocabulary, whilst others seem to have to rely on the arbitrary links between print and meaning that their visual memory allows. We (Dixon et al., 2002) set out to investigate whether these different ways of remembering words led to the formation of qualitatively different representations in sight vocabulary.

Phonemic identification and sight vocabulary

We worked again with 5-year-olds, and tested their ability to tell us what sounds spoken words began and ended with. We also again tested their knowledge of letter sounds. From these screening tests, we assigned the children to three groups. Children who could identify both initial and final phonemes and could select the letters to represent given phonemes at levels significantly above chance were assigned to group 1; children who could identify initial but not final phonemes, and could also select letters to represent given phonemes at levels significantly above chance were assigned to group 2; and children who could do neither phoneme identification task and were at chance on the sound-letter matching task were assigned to group 3. Chelsea, who could identify initial phonemes but not final phonemes (that is, could tell you that CAT begins with /k/, but not that CAT ends with /t/) and who by now had been taught lots of letter sounds, would have been assigned in this experiment to group 2.

We then set out again to teach some new words to all the children. But this time, we didn't just expect that group 1 would learn more quickly than group 2, who in turn would learn more quickly than group 3. This time we also predicted that children in the three different groups would store different representations of the words they learned. As children in group 1 were aware of sounds at both the beginning and end of words, we predicted that they would include the beginning and end letters of the word in their representation. Children in group 2 we thought would selectively store the beginning letter, and we didn't know what children in group 3, relying on visual memory rather than on forming links between some letters and some sounds, would store.

We made the learning task fearsomely difficult by making all ten words the same length, by printing them in capital letters so there were no overall distinguishing patterns of ascenders and descenders, and by having five pairs of words starting with the same letter. That is, we tried to teach SANDAL, SIGNAL, RASCAL, ROCKET, TICKET, TURNIP, CARTON, COBWEB, PICNIC, PENCIL. We showed the children the words on flashcards and we got them to match the words to pictures and we planned to continue this training until each child had read all ten words correctly in two consecutive sessions. But nine children, mostly from group 3, never met this criterion, and for such children training was stopped after 56 presentations of each word (14 training sessions).

Then we tested the children with the real words and a variety of misspelled versions of each, to discover which aspects of each word were represented in the child's memory for that word. We laid out a word and its seven variants on the table (for example, SANDAL PANDAL SANDAN SARDAL SANCAL NASDAL SANLAD SADNAL) and asked the child 'Which of these says "SANDAL"?' We noted which word the child chose and then asked, 'Do any of the others say "SANDAL"?' And we kept on noting the child's response and asking this question until the child said, no, none of the others was 'SANDAL'.

We expected children in group 1 to choose fewer variants of each word, because we expected them to have stored the first and last letter in their sight vocabulary representation. If this were so, then they would likely accept SANDAL SARDAL SANCAL SADNAL, that is, the real word and the three variants that retained the first and last letter. We were quite close here: on average, children in this group accepted 3.4 items, and were more likely to be misled by variants where the change was in the middle of the word.

We expected children in group 2 to choose more variants of each word than children in group 1, because we expected them to have stored only the first letter in their sight vocabulary representation. If this were so, then they would likely accept SANDAL SANDAN SARDAL SANCAL SANLAD SADNAL, that is, the real word and the five variants that retained the first letter. We were quite close here too: on average children in this group accepted 5.9 items, and only very seldom accepted variants where the first letter was wrong. And we expected children in group 3 to choose at random and possibly accept the real word and all its variants: they accepted on average 6.5 items, and were more likely than children in group 2 to accept variants where the first letter was wrong, although they were still less likely to accept variants where the first letter was wrong than variants with changes in other positions within the word. It clearly was a very hard task, and Chelsea might have commented, as did some of the children in groups 2 and 3: 'I know which ones say rocket, nearly all of them!' and 'But all of them look like turnip to me!'

Let's just pause here for a recap and think forward. Chelsea got off to a good start in reading because she knew about letters, she knew that spoken words were patterns of sounds, she could identify the initial sound in spoken words, she knew that sounds in words could be written with letters, and she knew the letters that stood for a few sounds. These attributes allowed her quickly to learn remaining letter–sound rules, and to use these to work out the pronunciations of some of the unfamiliar words she came across in reading texts. As we've seen, according to David Share the ability to sound out unfamiliar words acts as a self-teaching device: children who can use phonics to sound out unfamiliar words can then store these words in sight vocabulary for subsequent rapid recognition. Our experiments suggest that these attributes are what allowed Chelsea also to use her experiences in shared reading and in playing at reading to start to develop a sight vocabulary. Moreover, the representations she stored in sight vocabulary were likely to contain the first letter of each word, because as she could identify the first sound of the word, she could link the first letter to that sound, reducing the arbitrariness of the relationship between written word and meaning.

From initial and final phonemes to vowel digraphs: inferential self-teaching

How much better would Chelsea have done if she had also been able to identify the final sounds in spoken words? In that case, her sight vocabulary representations of words would include the first and last letters. That is, the word 'BOAT' would be represented as 'b–t', and the word 'NIGHT' as 'n–t'. From another of our experiments (Stuart et al., 1999), we argue that these skeletal representations provide the child with a particularly powerful device for learning.

So let's assume that by the time she was six (the age of the children in Stuart et al., 1999), Chelsea had got to grips with final sounds in words and was now storing both beginning and end letters in her sight vocabulary representations. If so, then as she reads and re-reads these words in the books she is now reading every day, in guided as well as shared reading sessions and at home with her parents, every repeat encounter with a word provides an opportunity to complete its representation in sight vocabulary. As she reads 'BOAT', the 'b' is already linked to /b/ and the 't' to /t/: the 'oa' must therefore link to the remaining portion of the sound pattern, to the /əʊ/ in the middle of /bəʊt/. As she reads 'NIGHT', the 'n' is already linked to /n/ and the t to /t/: the 'igh' must therefore link to the remaining portion of the sound pattern, to the /aɪ/ in the middle of /naɪt/. Chelsea aged six is able to learn further phonic rules from her experience of reading! Stuart et al. (1999) demonstrated this ability in 6- to 7-year-old readers who learned to read before the NLS was implemented. These children were taught only the sounds of single letters at school: no vowel digraphs were taught. We reasoned that if the children were nonetheless able to read made-up 'words' containing vowel digraphs correctly, they must have learned about the vowel digraphs from their reading experience, because nobody was directly teaching them these.

We used our database of the children's reading vocabulary to identify vowel digraphs that the children had come across very frequently (ee, ea) or very infrequently (oy, ei) in words they read in their school reading books. And as a check on our hypothesis that correct reading of vowel digraphs indicated self-teaching through reading, we further reasoned that children should in that case be more likely to read correctly the vowel digraphs they'd experienced frequently than those they'd not come across very often. So, in our experiment, 'ee' and 'ea' should be read correctly more often than 'oy' and 'ei'. But vowel digraphs differ in more than just frequency of occurrence: for example, they also differ in the consistency of their pronunciation. So we manipulated this too: 'ee' is always pronounced /i/ and 'oy' is always pronounced /ɔɪ/ in all the English words in which they occur; 'ea' and 'ei' are pronounced in a variety of ways in different words in English (bead, great, head; vein, heir, weird). So we also reasoned that consistency should affect vowel digraph reading accuracy: the consistent should be easier to learn than the inconsistent.

In this experiment, we split children into two groups, according to whether they were reading above or below the level expected for their age on a standardized word reading test. There was an effect of reader group: children reading at or above the expected level for their age were better at reading the vowel digraphs correctly. We also found the expected effect of vowel digraph frequency: 'ee' and 'ea' were read correctly much more often than 'oy' and 'ei'. Our scoring system militated against finding any effects of consistency, as we counted any of the several alternative pronunciations of each inconsistent digraph as correct.

The explanation I've given of how some children – 6- to 7-year-old children who are reading words well – might be able to learn further phonic rules from their experience of reading depends crucially on the notion that sight vocabulary representations which incorporate beginning and end letters of words provide opportunities for the child to infer that the remaining letters must represent the middle sound of the word. We found some support for this notion also, in that children who could identify the middle sound in a spoken word (that is, who could tell us that the middle sound in /baʊt/ was /aʊ/) were the best at reading vowel digraphs. The children with all the necessary prerequisites in place for such inferential learning to occur were indeed the best learners.

So, by the age of seven, Chelsea's ability to teach herself phonic rules from reading continues to increase the power of her phonic decoding abilities, so that she can sound out more and more complex words, which she can then store in sight vocabulary for future swift recognition. These two different kinds of word recognition processes (sight vocabulary; phonics) work together to reinforce and strengthen each other. Phonic knowledge allows rudimentary decoding of unfamiliar words and underpins early sight vocabulary; early sight vocabulary allows further phonic rules to be inferred; expansion of the phonic rule system allows more complex unfamiliar words to be decoded and stored as sight vocabulary; as sight vocabulary expands, so does the possibility for further inferences to be made; this further expands the phonic rule system and so on. This is why some children, like Chelsea, take to reading like ducks to water.

Systematic teaching of phonics

But what of the children who do not: how can they best be taught? First, we need to be able to identify such children early on. When we start teaching children to read, we need to know whether they are phonologically aware: whether they can identify rhymes and initial and final phonemes in spoken words. We need to know how many and which letter sounds they know. This information is quick and easy to obtain. It is probably counter-productive to start teaching children to read before they are capable of understanding and using the alphabetic principle. As Stuart et al. (2000) showed, children who are required to learn to read words before these capacities are developed rely on visual memory and are unable to do more than learn to associate arbitrary features of print with word meanings: this learning is unproductive and cannot generalize to novel items. Therefore, the first priority with 5-year-olds who are not phonologically aware and who do not know letter-sound correspondences is to teach them these things.

The research evidence clearly indicates that teaching phoneme awareness and phonics facilitates the development of word reading and spelling skills (for a review of the effects of phoneme awareness training, see Ehri et al., 2001b; for a review of the effects of phonics teaching, see Ehri et al., 2001a). In intervention studies with inner-city children, most of whom were learning English as an additional language (Stuart, 1999, 2004), children who were given one term of systematic phonics and phoneme awareness teaching in their second term in Reception were significantly better readers and spellers of words at the end of Year 1 than children not taught in this way. They retained their word reading and spelling advantage at the end of Year 2 over children in the sample who were not given any systematic phonics teaching throughout KS1. One class not taught systematic phonics in Reception had received one year of systematic phonics teaching during Year 2. This class were equally as good word readers as the Reception-taught group by the end of Year 2, although their ability to read 'made up' words (an analogue for 'unfamiliar words') was still less well developed than that of the children taught phonics for one term in Reception.

We also know that early systematic phonics teaching does not abolish individual differences: some children learn what is taught faster and with less need for practice than others. But it is clear that systematic phonics teaching which includes the two components of phoneme awareness and linking phonemes with letters is beneficial to the progress of children who learn with more difficulty and who need more practice (Hatcher et al., 2004).

If we adopt phoneme awareness and phonics teaching as the entry point for teaching reading, then many of the children we teach will, like Chelsea, get off to a flying start in reading and will progress, as Chelsea did, to develop a self-teaching system for reading words. This will be true even of some of those who enter school without the attributes that enabled Chelsea to get off to such a flying start, but who are quick to pick up on these things when they are given the opportunity to do so through structured, systematic and intensive teaching. The children who are slow to pick up on these things need more time and practice. For example, in the school where the *Jolly Phonics* programme was developed, the whole Reception class would go through the 10-week programme in the first term. Those who had not got it at the end of the first term were given additional small group teaching in the second term. Those who still had not got it then were given additional individual teaching in the third term. By the start of Year 1, the alphabetic principle was understood and used to some extent by all children. This, I suggest, is what we should be aiming to achieve for all the children we teach.

SOMETHING TO THINK ABOUT

- How do the arguments and evidence presented in this chapter relate to those in Chapter 6, 'Developmental Issues' and in Chapter 1, 'How Children Learn to Read'?

SOMETHING TO READ

- The author of this chapter was a member of the Rose Committee, which looked at the role of phonics in early reading. Read the Rose Review's report published in March 2006, available online at www.standards.dfes.gov.uk/rosereview/

SOMETHING TO DO

- Identify children in your class who bring some of the different kinds of understanding about sounds in words that are described in this chapter. Reflect on how well your current phonics curriculum is meeting their needs.

Chapter 3

Teaching Phonics:
The Basics

Sandra Farmer, Sue Ellis
and Vivienne Smith

> Unless you have phonemic awareness . . . it is impossible to gain much from instruction in phonics. (Harrison, 2004: 41)

Research about phonics for reading – and for spelling – exists in abundance. This chapter turns attention to the practical knowledge, skills and processes teachers, classroom assistants and student teachers need to embrace to teach phonics effectively. Interviews with practitioners and with tutors who provide continuing professional development courses consistently highlight the need for practitioners to have solid, practical understanding of the subject. Experienced phonics teachers will recognize much of the information in this chapter, and could use it when planning the content and activities for parents' workshops and induction sessions for new staff. The practicalities of how to teach a sequenced phonics programme are well covered in many commercial programmes and governmental resources, and such resources are easily accessible. This chapter therefore does not focus on the minutia of the order in which to teach phonemes, segmenting and blending, but rather on the fundamental understanding about these processes that practitioners must consider.

Talking about letters

When people begin working on phonics it is easy to make small and basic mistakes that create confusions for children. One basic mistake is confusing letter names and letter sounds. Children need to be taught quite clearly that letters have a *name* and make a *sound*. For some letters, the name and the sound are quite similar (the letter 'f', for example, makes the sound at the beginning of 'fish'). For others, the name and the sound are quite different (the letter 'c' makes the sound at the start of 'cat').

The complex orthography of English means that letters do not consistently make the same sounds (compare, for example, the 'c' in 'cat' and in 'circle' or the 's' in 'sea' and in 'sugar'). This can be confusing for children and needs to be acknowledged rather than ignored. It is particularly important to discuss it when children are doing activities such as the 'sound bag' or collecting objects beginning with a particular sound (perhaps to make a 'sound table'). Chapters 6 and 8 provide more detailed explanation of the complex relationship between sounds and letters in English.

Several phonics schemes begin by teaching children the sounds that letters make, and teach the letter names slightly later. This is fine unless children have already been taught the letter names at home or learned them from alphabet songs or watching popular television programmes such as *Sesame Street*. It is a good idea, when adults begin talking about letters, to ask the children what they already know. If the children already know the letter name, it makes sense to use this as an anchor for new knowledge about the sound. Otherwise, some children become confused, knowing lots of 'free-floating' bits of information about the letter but unsure of how it connects together and unable to use their knowledge effectively or confidently. Being able to link letter names and sounds is useful in other ways too. The important thing about letter names is that they are constant; the letter 'a' is always called 'a' but the sounds the letter 'a' can represent are numerous. Also, the letter names can help children to understand long vowels. Don't let children always associate letter names with upper-case writing and sounds with lower-case writing.

Making sounds

When you say 'sounds', be careful not to distort the sound by enunciating in an exaggerated way. It is especially important to avoid adding an extra 'uh' (technically called a 'schwa' sound) to the consonant; try to say 'c', 'rrr' and 't' rather than 'cuh', 'ruh' and tuh'. Some sounds are running sounds like aaaa, rrrrrrrrr, lllllllllll, mmmmmm, nnnnnnnn and ssssss and are fairly easy to articulate without the intrusive 'schwa', but c, t, b, p, g are much harder and are notoriously vulnerable to over-articulation or vocalizing a vowel at the end. The sound that 'c' makes can, with care, run on. Other consonants, however, especially those known as the plosives (e.g. b and p) are much trickier. Sometimes it helps to separate a sound by rapidly repeating it in its briefest form – b b b b b b.

Over-enunciation of isolated sounds interferes with children's understanding of how to blend sounds, segment sounds and listen for sounds.

Don't assume that children understand the words you use

It seems obvious to check that the children know what you mean when you use terminology such as 'word', 'letter' and 'sound'. Young children may not have had a lot of previous discussion about the mechanics of print and may not be completely secure about what these terms mean. Even experienced teachers can make assumptions about the vocabulary and experiences children bring.

Words such as 'beginning', 'middle' and 'end' can also cause confusion. Some children may still be struggling to use 'beginning', 'middle' and 'end' easily when talking about physical objects that they can see and touch. Spoken words are far harder – they are transitory: they cannot be seen and they cannot be touched. When children first learn to talk, they think of words solely in terms of what they mean: for a young child 'ice lolly' is often one word (because it relates to one thing) and it means, quite simply, an ice lolly. It must seem very strange to children unused to thinking of words as a sequence of sounds or articulatory movements, to suddenly hear their teacher talking about an 'ice lolly' as two words, each with a 'beginning' and an 'end'. Hatcher (2000) and Adams et al. (1998) offer some practical advice for helping children to hear the sounds.

Don't confuse phonemes with letters

Experience has shown that adults often discern small units better, not in sound but in writing. There is an irony here, for teachers often bemoan the fact that children do not listen very well. Classroom experience shows that children are able to discern phonemes aurally once they have reached the phoneme-chunking stage of phonological development (see Chapter 8). Adults, by contrast, are often almost irretrievably immersed in visual, print-borne information and find it difficult to focus on hearing the sounds rather than seeing the letters. One of the most basic mistakes adults make in teaching phonics, therefore, is that their knowledge of the letters used in the written word overrides their ability to hear the number of actual sounds in it.

For example, take the word 'cat'. Say the word slowly and smoothly, stretching out the sounds to let them run easily into each other. Count how many different sounds you say in the word. Adults generally have no trouble identifying three sounds (or phonemes) – 'c', 'a' and 't'. You will note that the number of phonemes in the word 'cat' matches the number of letters. However, now do the same exercise for 'chat'. You should find that 'chat' has the same number of phonemes as 'cat' but a different number of letters: the first phoneme in 'chat' is 'ch', a single sound but represented by two letters – a digraph.

The following activity will help practitioners to find out for themselves the extent to which they have a secure and explicit awareness of phoneme (sound)

	Number of phonemes (sounds) in the word	Number of letters in the word	Digraphs (two letters that make one sound)	Trigraphs (three letters that make one sound)	Quadragraphs (four letters that make one sound)
Cat	3	3	–	–	–
Chat	3	4	ch	–	–
Splat					
Bridge					
Catch					
Clock					
Caught					

Table 3.1 Working out how phonemes relate to graphemes in words

and grapheme (letter(s) that represent the sound) boundaries. Consider in turn each of the words in Table 3.1. Say each word slowly and smoothly. As you say the words, listen very carefully for the different phonemes you hear and count them. Beware! You may have a tendency to see the letters of the word rather than hear the changes in sound as the word is said. Compare your answers with those of a colleague before reading the next paragraph.

You should have found that 'splat' has five phonemes (and five letters); 'bridge' has four phonemes ('b' 'r' 'i' 'j') and six letters. 'Catch' has three phonemes ('c' 'a' 'ch' – note that the final phoneme is exactly the same as the first sound in 'chat') but it has five letters, whereas 'clock', also with five letters, has four phonemes ('c' 'l' 'o' 'c').

An understanding of how sounds are articulated can help to stop adults being blinded by the number of letters in a word (see Chapter 6). Various practical approaches can support people in listening to the phonemes in a word, rather than looking at the letters. Miskin (2005) recommends counting the phonemes by stretching each sound along a separate finger whilst saying the word slowly and smoothly. Marie Clay recommends using Elkonin boxes, where empty squares represent the number of phonemes in the word. The word is pronounced slowly and smoothly (stretched-out) and counters placed in the appropriate square as each new phoneme is heard (Clay, 1993: 33). It is also helpful if children are taught to write digraphs, trigraphs and quadragraphs in flowing, joined script from the start to emphasize the link with the sound and establish automatic spelling patterns.

It is critical that practitioners feel very secure in their concepts of phonemes and graphemes and their boundaries. Why? Because this marks the difference between phonics teaching of the past and what has been referred to as 'new phonics'. Old phonics teaching tended to assume blending as an obvious and automatic process, and blended sounds were often taught as a unit. (For example, children would be asked to look for 'sp' in the beginning of words such as 'spell', the end of words such as 'wasp' and in the middle of words such as 'raspberry'). Thus, old phonics teaching approaches didn't consistently take sounds down to the basic unit of the phoneme. The 'new phonics' approach argues that this is important; children must be taught to hear and understand phonemes if they are to understand the alphabetic principle (Bielby, 1994).

Be clear about whether you are teaching onset–rime or CVC words

Many practitioners have 'picked up' terms such as 'onset and rime' and 'CVC words' but haven't necessarily thought about how the two relate to each other. When practitioners are teaching using onset and rime, the teaching activity should involve isolating all the consonants at the beginning of a syllable up to the first vowel. This is the onset. The first vowel and any remaining vowels and consonants are the rime. For example cl/ock are the onset and rime for clock, w/ig-w/am are the onsets and rimes for the two-syllable word 'wigwam'. Teaching activities using onset and rime involve children in listening to these sounds. Having identified these sounds, teachers then often ask children to analyse the visual patterns of the letters and use this information to work out new words. For example, the rime 'ock' helps children work out dock, lock, sock and so on. Hearing onset and rime and seeing letter patterns are not inevitably bound together, however (see Chapter 1 for a fuller discussion).

When practitioners teach CVC words, they are often teaching children to hear and identify all the individual phonemes in the word, in sequence. The tasks tend to involve activities such as blending individual phonemes to make a whole word or separating a whole word into its constituent sounds.

It is not a bad idea to use the technical terms with children, as long as this doesn't confuse them. The important thing to remember is that the activities associated with onset–rime and with CVC words require different kinds of thinking about the sounds and the relationship between sounds and letters; both are valid and important for different reasons. Chapter 2 explains the importance of teaching CVC words and Chapter 8 explains the importance of acknowledging letter strings that do not fit the principle of matching one phoneme (sound) per letter.

Take a critical look at activities and worksheets

To use phonics effectively, children must be taught to hear the phonemes in words, to hear the sequence of phonemes and to know and be able to write the letters and letter combinations that commonly represent those phonemes in written English.

We all know that teachers must actively teach and cannot expect activities and worksheets to do the job for them. Some activities and worksheets may give opportunities to clarify understandings and to practise and consolidate knowledge. To be sure of this, however, practitioners need to look analytically at the talking and the thinking that the worksheet or activity promotes in practice. There are several drawbacks to using worksheets as the mainstay of a phonics programme. One is that 'doing' the worksheet often involves spending less than a minute thinking about the sounds and the letters; the bulk of the time is spent colouring in the pictures. Another potential problem is that many phonics worksheets can be completed purely on the basis of visual information; the child can correctly match-up similar letters without ever thinking about how the word sounds, how it is articulated or connecting the phonemes with the letters that represent them. A third issue is that to illustrate sounds, worksheets sometimes assume a vocabulary that is simply not within the modern child's experience. A recent example was children from an economically disadvantaged Glasgow estate completing a worksheet about the phoneme 'i'. Two of the four objects used to illustrate this sound were 'ink' (the illustration was of a traditional ink bottle) and 'imp' (the illustration showed a pixie-type figure). Imps and the ink required for traditional fountain pens not being familiar objects, these children were talking about a 'bottle' and a 'wee man'. They saw no relationship between the phoneme 'i' and the objects depicted on the worksheet. Although they enjoyed colouring the pictures, one has to question what they learned about phonics. They would have benefited more from the kinds of explicit, interactive teaching described in Chapter 4, firmly embedded in illustrations of how and why this knowledge is useful and encouragement to use it in reading and writing activities across the curriculum.

Understand the technical terms and don't be afraid to use them

Crucial to any exploration of phonics for teachers, teaching assistants and other practitioners is the need to clarify the core concepts and terminology used. Spend a few moments thinking about how you would complete each of the following sentence starters. Try to capture the essence of each term by jotting down key words and phrases:

- Phonics is . . .
- Phonemic awareness is . . .
- Phonological awareness is . . .
- Phonetics is . . .

Invite other colleagues to engage in this task and share your comments. A useful starting point is to consider which of the four terms felt least threatening – or most familiar – to each of you, as well as what you have each written down.

Discuss how you felt when trying to differentiate these terms. Many teachers, students and teaching assistants report an uncomfortable level of inadequacy, even embarrassment. This often leads to consideration of the importance of open discussion and direct training in both initial teacher education and subsequent professional development courses.

A glance down the list shows that all the four terms share the same stem *phon* – linking them all in some way to *sound*. A focus on the term 'phonics', however, cannot solely encompass sound, but also the association between a sound and the symbol(s) used to depict that sound in writing. Teachers may be familiar with educational psychologists' reports which sometimes refer to 'sound to symbol' and 'symbol to sound' processing. This kind of language is more accurate than 'sound to letter' and 'letter to sound' processing. The moment we make reference to the symbolic information of writing we move into 'graphic' rather than 'phonic' information. Hence it seems that the term 'phonics' is better understood as a shorthand term for either 'grapho-phonics' (if the literacy process is reading) or 'phono-graphics' (if the literacy process is spelling/writing). Now our original terms have multiplied. We have:

- phonological awareness
- phonics
- graphological awareness
- graphics

Let's move now to 'phonological awareness' – usefully interpreted as a lifelong development centred on the ability to 'chunk' for sound. For a detailed description of how children develop phonological awareness and what this involves, see Chapter 6. Suffice to say that phonological awareness is an umbrella term covering a range of increasingly finely-tuned developments, underpinned by the ever-more conscious awareness of, and ability to manipulate, the sounds of language. A high level of phonological awareness is the ability to engage in spoonerisms: turning 'car park' into 'par cark' and 'cat-nap' into 'nat-cap', for example.

So what, then, is the difference between phonological awareness and phonemic awareness? It is useful here to consider phonemic awareness as a vital stage in the overall development of phonological awareness. Within the term 'phonemic' is the notion of a phoneme. A phoneme is the smallest unit of sound in language that changes meaning. Take the word 'cat' – change the initial sound from 'c' to 'th' or 'f' and the meaning of the original word is changed; change the middle sound to 'u' or 'o' and 'cat' becomes 'cut' or 'cot'; change the final sound to 'p' or 'ch' and 'cat' becomes 'cap' or 'catch'. Phonemic awareness, therefore, is the conscious understanding that words are made up of individual sounds (phonemes) and that these sounds are represented through the alphabet. Activities that require phonemic awareness include alliteration, 'spot the odd one out' tasks, phoneme segmentation, phoneme blending and phoneme manipulation.

Phonetics concerns the articulation and acoustic features of speech sounds. Articulatory phonetics explains the distinction between consonants and vowels (see Chapter 6) and can help listeners identify the phonemic pattern of words.

Parallel distinctions exist for talking about knowledge of the written letters. Thus, a grapheme is the smallest unit of written language that changes the meaning of a word and graphemic awareness, the awareness, sensitivity to and ability to manipulate graphemes to change the meaning of a word.

Make the purpose and applications of phonics lessons explicit

Everyone learns more effectively when they understand how the learning will be useful and can link the learning activity they have been set with wider, more general experiences. This matters because children need to apply new knowledge many times before it moves from working memory to long-term memory and becomes effortless and automatic.

Sometimes links that seem obvious to practitioners are less obvious to children, who often 'ring-fence' knowledge and see it as only applicable to particular activities or situations (Guthrie, 2004). Thus, the links between phonics lessons, reading and writing need to be demonstrated and followed through to make the wider applications completely explicit. Children need to be shown how phonics is useful, and this must be integral to the teaching session, rather than an 'afterthought' at the end of the lesson or a separate lesson. It also means that children should be coached in using their knowledge during real-life writing and reading tasks, not just on games, worksheets and activities.

It is always good practice to ask children to suggest when they will be able to use and apply what they have learnt: it helps to make the links explicit, encourages a disposition for seeing links and encourages children to take responsibility for, and notice opportunities for, their own learning. Incidental comments by adults are also a powerful influence on the learning ethos in class. Teachers and classroom assistants who point out and encourage children to apply their learning to new activities, and who notice and compliment children when they spontaneously make such links, help create this ethos.

Don't 'over-teach': keep lessons pacy, interactive and personally relevant

Teaching that is too pedestrian and earnest lacks impact. Short, pacy and frequent phonics inputs have more impact than longer, drawn-out sessions

(Ofsted, 2005d). It is important to link new sounds to those that children already know, but if lessons lack variety and if whole class teaching means that children have to re-visit and re-explain old ideas too often, they become bored and switch off. Multisensory approaches that include visual, auditory and kinaesthetic ways of learning are important. For example, letters can be said, chanted and sung about, their shapes can be created through body and hand movements and they can be seen in different fonts and sizes. Multisensory teaching supports all learners, including dyslexic children. Such approaches help secure learning in long-term memory and support learners in making that learning 'automatic' (PNS, 2005; Augur and Briggs, 1992). Varied resources such as wooden, plastic and magnetic letters in an alphabet arc promote graphemic and phonemic awareness.

It is also important to consider the social and emotional dimension of learning. For adults, a letter is simply a letter and a sound simply a sound, but young children are different. Some letters, and some sounds, are far more important and salient than others, and the most important of all are those in their own names and in the names of those they love. Many phonics schemes advocate a teaching sequence based on introducing the most useful, high-frequency phonemes first and in fairly quick succession to allow children to combine and use them in writing and reading. For younger children, however, it may be effective to introduce the letters and sounds that make 'emotional sense' at this early stage, when they can become a useful anchor for other learning.

Be a 'noticing' practitioner

There is much emphasis on and encouragement for schools to introduce whole class phonics instruction as early as possible. For children who are able to hear and manipulate phonemes this appears be a good thing. However, some groups of children have particular problems with blending and segmenting sounds. These include children who stammer, children with 'glue-ear' and other types of hearing loss (temporary or permanent), as well as any children who lack the requisite level of phonemic or phonological awareness. Younger children are particularly vulnerable in this respect. They will often benefit more from playful opportunities to share and enjoy the sounds and rhythms of language than from a highly structured and inflexible phonics programme at this stage.

Practitioners need to ensure that the relentless pace of whole class teaching does not put such children under undue pressure. It is important to quickly notice and respond to difficulties, and to recognize that support for such a child may involve *less* emphasis on a phonics programme and more emphasis on the alternative ways into reading and writing which are part of a broad literacy curriculum (see Chapter 4).

Make the phonics worthwhile

Decoding words is not an end in itself. In an analysis of lift-the-flap books, Vivienne Smith (2003) shows how the books children read teach them not only about reading but also about learning. When children read meaningful, engaging and playful texts, and when they read widely and discuss what the texts mean for them and their lives, children become adventurous, thoughtful and active readers. They also learn, in Smith's words, that 'knowledge is open-ended and the omniscience of the text is limited' (2003: 121). Similarly, when children are encouraged to write about matters that are important to them and can write freely, using their writing to reach out to the reader and to invite the reader into their world and their thoughts, they become articulate, reflective authors. Unless children are shown how to put their phonic knowledge to powerful use, all will come to nought. As Mark Twain is quoted as saying, 'Those who don't read have no advantage over those who can't.'

SOMETHING TO THINK ABOUT

- How can teachers and teaching assistants encourage children to apply newly learned phonic knowledge immediately and repeatedly so that they develop automaticity in terms of transferring and applying phonics across a range of tasks and subjects?
- How is children's progress monitored in your school? In particular, how quickly are children who don't seem to be making sense of phonics instruction noticed, and what types of support are they offered?

SOMETHING TO READ

- Kathy Hall (see Chapter 1) and Colin Harrison (2004) will help practitioners locate phonics teaching within the wider domain of reading. Harrison, C. (2004) *Understanding Reading Development*. London: Sage.

- Adams, M.J., Foorman, B., Lundberg, I. and Beeler, T. (1998) *Phonemic Awareness in Young Children*. Baltimore MD. Paul, H. Brookes. This book builds up children's phonological development through a series of carefully structured yet fun-packed games.

SOMETHING TO DO

- Listen carefully to two or more people talking together. Really listen to the sounds they are saying – especially the way words merge (for example, people actually say 'dwa' for 'do our' in the sentence 'we're going to do our homework').
- Be more sensitive to the range of ways people in school speak – especially dialect differences and variations in accent. Drawing children's attention to the different ways that a word is enunciated can help to make the sound structures in words more conspicuous.
- Encourage children to count phonemes and graphemes carefully and consider teaching a joined script to write the letters of digraphs, trigraphs or quadragraphs.

Chapter 4

Inside the Classroom: Three Approaches to Phonics Teaching

*Lyndsay Macnair, Sally Evans,
Margaret Perkins and Prue Goodwin*

In all the debates about the role of phonics and the kind of phonics we should use, it is important to consider what the different approaches to phonics means in terms of classroom practice. What are the teaching and learning experiences, and what are the outcomes for children who are taught by practitioners with different beliefs about the teaching of phonics?

In the first part of this chapter a teacher who first used synthetic phonics in Clackmannanshire describes how she now mixes the approach with more writing and play-based activities in her current school in Stirling. In the second part, a teacher describes how she uses both synthetic and analytic phonics in her class. The final account describes a heavily integrated and contextualized approach based on exploring language in many ways.

Synthetic Phonics – How I Teach It

Lyndsay Macnair

I have taught phonics to infants in Scotland and New Zealand but I first became aware of a new approach to teaching phonics whilst I was teaching in England. Former colleagues in Clackmannanshire were piloting a synthetic phonics programme and were keen to share their success. I spoke at length with my former colleagues and had opportunities to observe lessons. On my return to teaching in

Clackmannanshire I was formally introduced to the Council's synthetic phonics programme with in-service training sessions and lesson observations.

From these sessions my first impression was that of speed. The pace of the lesson was very slick and well structured. Letters and sounds were introduced with up to four new sounds a week, which was much quicker than any approach I had previously experienced. The children were being exposed to vocabulary such as 'vowel' and 'consonant' right from the start, with the use of colour and flags to differentiate between the two. They were encouraged to look for letters and state their position in a word, be it beginning, middle or end. Children were active and interacting in the lessons: finding letters, blending words and forming letters. The children's enthusiasm and sense of achievement was electric and impressed me greatly.

My second observation was the variety of resources used. These included flashcards, invaluable magnetic letters on individual boards as well as a magnetic wedge with the alphabet along the top, all within one lesson. I cannot stress how important the magnetic boards and letters were. The children were able to work in pairs and individually to blend words. The letters were introduced onto the boards as they were taught. This was a resource idea I took away, used and adapted.

Having observed lessons and read the teachers' material I was keen to begin. I started with a small class and developed a blueprint which I now use with most classes I teach. The most important point to stress is that the children's active participation in the lesson is key to its success. They must be able to access the whiteboard, chalkboard or wedge – whichever I am using – so I have the children sitting in front of the chalkboard in rows or in a circle with the magnetic boards within reach. I have placed a grid overlay on the magnetic boards, containing the letters of the alphabet, with the vowels highlighted in red. The children are responsible for adding new letters and putting the letters back on the grid when they have finished. I have also invested in a wooden set of magnetic letters which have the vowels highlighted in another colour. This avoids any mix-ups with magnetic letters when the children use the large board.

A typical phonics session

A typical phonics lesson lasts approximately 30–40 minutes and is split into roughly six parts:

- *Warm-up* begins with oral starter activities which include the alphabet song, the name game, letters before and after, and 'vowel owls'.
- *Revision* of previous teaching using letter flashcards and magnetic wedge. The children identify and say the letters and do the actions as the flashcards are shown. This is reinforced again by asking the children to find letter sounds on the wedge. The children are then asked to read words from the board that reinforce the previous letters taught. At this point I get the children to rub the words off the board as they read them (which gives great

satisfaction). Included on the board are the tricky words, which the children learn alongside the letter sounds. I also have a selection of words as flashcards. These are stuck to the board and collected instead of being rubbed off. The children are given an opportunity to spell words. At this point I remind them that to read a word they need to sound and blend it. The children help me write words on the board sounding out each letter in turn reinforcing beginning, middle and end. The children then make words using their magnetic letters.

- *A new sound* is then taken from the alphabet and shown to the children with the explanation that the letter makes a particular sound. At this point an action is introduced to help the children remember the sound for that letter. The children are then shown the printed version of the letter on the flashcard as well as the written version on the board and wedge. Words containing the new sound are written on the board and a volunteer is asked to find the new sound, circle it and say its position in the word either beginning, middle or end. I then ask for examples of words containing the new sound and write them on the board, or the child can write them on the board with the help of their peers. The children are asked to put the word into the context of a sentence.

- *Word making* with the magnetic letters to reinforce the new sound is always popular with the children. Words are given and the children have to locate the letter for each sound and place them in the correct order at the bottom of their boards starting at the left-hand side, which is marked with a star. This is an opportunity for paired working, when the children can assist each other.

- *Letter formation* is practised with magic finger pencil writing on the floor, a leg or in the air. Volunteers are asked to come and write on the board. The children are shown a cursive font from the start, as we encourage cursive handwriting at my school. I use individual whiteboards for this, giving children the opportunity to make errors without worrying about its finality. The children are then asked to assess their work and circle the best example, and I do the same. These boards can be photocopied for evidence when required.

- *Consolidation* is completed in the form of a game, a written activity, a whiteboard activity or a reading activity. I try to have a blank sound board on the go for that day, giving the children a chance to add words containing the new sound throughout the day, circling the sound for the day. If the child cannot spell the word, I help them to sound it out. I often challenge the children to find more words than the day before. This is a fun way to learn and the children especially enjoy playing the games. These include picture cue cards, a game which the child takes and makes the word either with the magnetic letters or the whiteboard. Pairs matching words to pictures also helps to develop memory skills. The children really enjoy sitting in a circle with a mountain of words in front of them. They are timed to collect as many words as they can read. If they are stuck they can put the word back or seek peer or teacher help. This can be differentiated by placing the harder words in front of the more confident child, saving simpler words for the less confident. It's the sense of achievement that is important in this game.

The impact of the approach

Having taught phonics for a number of years, I was surprised at the speed and eagerness with which the children approached reading. The rate at which the children progressed through the reading scheme as well as their hunger for non-fiction material was impressive. They were willing to try the strategies shown during the phonics lessons on everything. They were displaying competent word attack skills and as a result new words were not daunting but rather a challenge to be overcome. This had a huge impact on the rest of my teaching. The children were able to write independently very early on and were confident in their writing. They were unfazed by new vocabulary. They sounded words out and wrote them down; yes, phonetically spelled, but nonetheless the children were writing and were not afraid to have a go. The spelling improved as their knowledge base grew. The amount the children wrote also increased, as did the range of contexts they wrote about. The children's handwriting improved as the children were exposed to the cursive formation of letters right from the beginning, and when digraphs were taught the children wrote them with the joins in place, knowing no different.

Environmental topics were now more challenging; the children in Primary 1 (who entered the class aged four and a half to five and a half) were able to complete simple research activities I had previously introduced in Primary 2, such as finding key vocabulary and facts from non-fiction material. The children were also able to transfer the knowledge gained from research when compiling their Jungle Journals, writing at least three facts about a variety of grassland and jungle animals. Citizenship also benefited as the children were keen to write more in their class journals after visits home or to interesting places. The children were also able to read the journal themselves.

An added bonus was that of peer support. The children were able to help one another and to read what each other had written. We made time for sharing writing with our friends and classmates. Teaching synthetic phonics had a huge impact not only on the class but also on the rest of the school and the parents.

I was aware that this approach to phonics was new to many parents. Many felt it alien to them and were concerned about 'not teaching it right'. As a result the parents were invited to attend workshops within the school and in the class, where they were shown a typical phonics lesson to help them develop a clearer understanding of the strategies and expressions used. It was also an opportunity for the teacher to dispel any parental concerns or confusion in a friendly informal way. The parents were shown a range of the activities and games that the children completed on a weekly basis. Many were surprised by the capability and confidence of their child.

Within the school there were implications for the management team as well as fellow teachers. Provision of resources and training had to be sustained as the approach was rolled out throughout the infant department and beyond. The attainment of the children had to be recognized and developed. These children needed to be challenged at every opportunity or they would become bored and lose their enthusiasm. This had implications for teaching and resources. The children had to be given activities that were stimulating as well as challenging. The management had to monitor this and encourage staff to look beyond familiar 'stage appropriate' resources and schemes and provide support to adapt resources and make them appropriate to the needs of the child. This included providing wider reading material to complement the existing reading 'scheme' material. Benchmarks in writing were constantly evaluated, looking to develop and improve upon the year before.

Phonics, like most lessons, has to be fun and interactive to be remembered. Within my career I have witnessed a number of approaches to teaching phonics become popular only to be overtaken by the next latest and greatest. I have been fortunate to participate in this Synthetic Phonics approach which I have tried, tested, refined and believe will stand the test of time. In my opinion the measure of its success is the joyful expressions of a class of children reading a new book for the first time or a piece of writing to a friend.

A Commentary on Practices in the Synthetic Phonics Classroom, by the Editors

Some of the practices mentioned in this account will be familiar in many classrooms, whatever form of phonics teaching is adopted: an emphasis on active teaching and learning; an expectation that all children will engage; the use of familiar games and routines; the employment of visual, aural and kinaesthetic ways of learning; the linking of reading and writing and the eagerness of the young learners to participate. There are also familiar games and practices, such as the parallel learning of phonemes and their graphemes and the use of letters to aid word building. The correct naming of vowels and consonants and encouraging children to pay explicit attention to letter position is also common practice in many classrooms.

Readers will, however, be struck by the heightened pace of the introduction of new sounds (up to four a week) and the amount of time given to phonic teaching (30–40 minutes per day). This is in line with an approach that sees synthetic phonics as a 'fast and first approach'. At this rate all the phonemes can be introduced within a term. The literacy session concentrates on teaching and practising the phonemes and blending them to make words. Little time in this session appears to be given to reading sentences or extended prose. The use of decodable books is not specifically mentioned in this account but is often promoted as part of more radical synthetic phonics programmes. Proponents of synthetic phonics advocate giving children books they can read, which involves restricting the vocabulary to the phonemes taught. There is also no use of segmenting words to help children see letter patterns and draw analogies to help with spelling and reading other words.

The phonic sessions are structured into a familiar routine – just as the literacy hour in England follows a fairly fixed structure. Such a regular routine can be supportive of learners as they know what to expect; routines help to establish a community of learners and so the social practices adopted in this classroom are taken as the norm by the children. The teacher's commitment to the programme comes through clearly. Such commitment is likely to impact on outcomes. The teacher's commitment was strengthened by professional development support.

A Mixed Approach: Synthetic and Analytic Phonics Within a Broad Literacy Curriculum

Sally Evans

My phonics teaching is based around *Playing with Sounds: A Supplement to Progression in Phonics* (DfES, 2003a). This programme is produced by the Primary National Strategy/National Literacy Strategy. My phonics teaching is only part of my wider approach to the teaching of literacy, but I understand that teaching phonics is an important element in learning to read and I give it regular time in the literacy hour.

My phonics teaching is planned, regular and structured. It is also fun and active. It includes opportunities for children to use their phonic knowledge, such as noticing sounds, words and patterns as we read books together for pleasure and meaning. These shared reading books may be beyond those the children could read unaided. In guided reading the books will be at an instructional level of difficulty. An excited voice calling 'Miss, Miss. Look it's a "ch",' or 'There are three "ing" words on that page' as we enjoy a class Big Book or a guided reading session is a regular occurrence.

I see phonics as important but I do not see it as the only strategy my pupils need. At the same time as we are learning and using phonics I introduce children to other strategies they can use to help them read and understand a book, such as learning high-frequency words as sight vocabulary, using picture cues, reading on and using the context and syntax to work out what is a likely or unlikely word.

My pupils come from a range of different cultural communities and have different experiences of exposure to books and awareness of environmental print. They have a variety of knowledge about language patterns, letter sounds and the alphabet letter names through the things they have done at home and during their time in a variety of pre-school education settings and reception class. Some of my children speak English as an additional language. By the time they start in Year 1 there are noticeable differences in all childrens' attitudes towards learning to read and the early reading skills they have already acquired. This means that I need to differentiate for various groups and individuals. Although I plan for the *Playing with Sounds* (DfES, 2003a) programme as a class, there are some groups and individuals who may need to spend more time within literacy sessions, practising and applying new phonic knowledge, and others who are capable of moving on quickly. I have an experienced classroom assistant who has developed her own knowledge of phonics through working closely with me and through running National Literacy Strategy intervention programmes such as *Early Literacy Support* (DfEE, 1999b), and so one of us will take a group that needs additional coaching. For the 'average' child I expect them to leave Year 1 as well established beginning readers with a knowledge of the high-frequency words listed in the framework, a sound understanding of the alphabetic code and able to decode phonemically regular words. I expect them to segment words and recognize patterns in words and use this to help with reading and spelling. I also aim to ensure that they see the pleasures and purposes of reading and writing, see themselves as readers and writers, and have a range of strategies as well as phonics that they can use to help them as they read.

The literacy environment

My literacy teaching starts with the classroom environment. There are plenty of attractive books (fiction and non-fiction) and a comfortable carpeted area where we gather to read, as a class, a group or individually. There are posters, alphabet friezes, labelled displays, word walls and labelled resources, all of which create a print-rich environment. I have lots of language resources, including phonic resources such as games, magnetic, felt and wooden letters and individual whiteboards for children to 'have a go'. The role-play area is set up to provide a context in which they can see and use reading and writing (and mathematics). This half-term we have a hospital, last term we had our Fairy Tale Cottage where a notice on the door saying *Just gone for a walk* turned it into the Three Bears' cottage, one saying *Lift up the latch and walk in* turned it into Grandma's cottage, a royal invitation in the letter box turned it into Cinderella's kitchen and so on. There are always writing materials in this area and the children use their phonic knowledge as they write out a shopping list for mummy bear or a 'do not disturb' notice for Grandma's door. We have a puppet theatre with a range of puppets including a 'Word Wizard'. Word Wizard's cloak was made by one of our parents and has letters scattered over it. Word Wizard takes part in many of our phonic games and attempts at blending and segmenting. He's very good at these and can help, prompt and demonstrate. We also have 'Baby Word Wizard' (who has a different coloured cloak and an L-plate) who often gets things wrong or gets stuck. The children love helping him out.

I use ICT constantly to support and encourage reading. This includes things such as phonic games on the computer, electronic Big Books, writing our own books based on digital photographs that children add captions to and so on. I have many everyday uses of ICT that support literacy. For example, when the children enter the classroom in the morning and sit on the carpet, the computer is running a programme that runs the words 'Hello Isha, Hello James . . .' (through all the names of the class) along the bottom of the interactive whiteboard. As they settle down they look out for their name and their friends' names. As the year progresses the message becomes longer – 'Good morning' or 'How are you today?' The children are thrilled when a new message appears and read it with great excitement.

Typical phonic sessions

So what does a typical week of phonics teaching look like in my classroom? Most days start with some songs, nursery rhymes or a language game as we gather on the carpet. For some children these reinforce their phonemic awareness, for others they are essential in continuing to give them vital early language experiences they still need. Each day we have a literacy session of about an hour. We spend about 15 minutes on word level work, and three or four times a week this will be dedicated wholly to phonic work. It will often begin with a song such as 'Vowel Rap' or the 'OO Song' and then I will introduce a new sound or sounds that we will draw on our neighbour's back and on our whiteboards as we say it aloud. I will write a word containing the phoneme and we will segment it into all its phonemes. We will put it with other phonemes we know (using magnetic letters or the interactive whiteboard) to blend into a word. We write the word and we will generate other words with the same pattern. Children will try writing these on their whiteboards. I introduce phonemes in an ordered way – initial, final and medial – and we differentiate between consonants and vowels. We will play a game using the sound(s), perhaps with our letter fans or on the interactive whiteboard. We often create a sentence or two, which I scribe and which the children read back to me. As the year progresses they write their own sentences.

I often start the literacy session with this word level work before moving on to some shared reading or writing where children have further opportunities to apply their phonic knowledge. During the independent group work some groups will do further phonic practice through more games or through intensive work with an adult. As well as the word level time within the literacy session, playing around with sounds is threaded through short activities throughout the day. For example, I may ask the children to line up in a certain order depending on phonemes – all those whose name begins with 'm', with 'b'; in PE we make the shapes of letters as a warm-up activity, running round the hall and then making a Y or a T or whatever.

Another word level session in the week will have a quick recap and revisit of what we have done in phonics up to that point, but will then focus on sight vocabulary and vocabulary extension. Handwriting is integrated into all the word level sessions as we create letter shapes, but further handwriting activities are undertaken at other times during the week too.

My long-term phonics planning is based on the medium-term plans provided on the *Playing with Sounds* CD-ROM. This takes most children through all the seven steps of *Progression in Phonics* by the end of term 1. The steps have also been modified to introduce some vowels earlier so that the children can blend words at an early stage. This is faster than the original pace suggested by

Progression in Phonics in 1999, but the introduction to *Playing with Sounds* explains that this is because research shows that most children can progress at this faster rate. The day-to-day phonic activities are taken from the many suggestions on the laminated cards of the programme. These cards (22 in all) progress systematically from such things as enjoying rhyming and rhythmic activity to vowel digraphs and reading long words by identifying the phonemes in syllables. The first 15 or so cards are aimed at foundation stage but are very useful for tracking back for those children who need further experiences in these early steps. There are screening materials for early identification of children who may need additional support in phoneme-grapheme correspondences, blending, segmenting and decoding.

The cards also offer me professional development support as each step has an introductory card that gives advice on:

- early learning goals/learning objectives;
- what children need to have experienced;
- explanation of any terminology;
- what I need to know about this step (the professional content knowledge the teacher needs to understand); and
- assessing children's development.

In the three years since I began teaching I have learnt a huge amount about the role of phonics. Every day I see how it helps my children to read and to write, but I do not think it works in isolation; it is part of a broader package.

A Commentary on the Mixed Approach Classroom, by the Editors

Many of the activities described above are similar to those described in the 'synthetic phonics classroom', but simultaneously with the phonic teaching there is work on sight vocabulary, other reading cues and supported reading and enjoyment of books beyond the child's reading ability. In guided reading sessions children would be encouraged to use phonics to read unknown words, but they would also be reminded of other strategies that can help them. There is a different pace of phonics teaching in this class – although still fast – and a different amount of time given to it. Emphasis is also given to using letter patterns.

This teacher integrates phonics with the wider literacy curriculum and sees phonics as one skill to be developed and used among others, not as a completely distinct skill to be taught separately and first. Like the synthetic phonics teacher, this teacher plays short games to reinforce phonic knowledge, offering children lots of kinaesthetic and interactive opportunities to learn. Also like the synthetic phonics teacher, she actively encourages children to use their phonic knowledge across the literacy curriculum – to recognize their names on the computer, to write and to help her compose writing on the interactive whiteboard. She too has had professional development support and has this confirmed by the information on the introduction to the cards and by supporting videos.

Play and Planning: A Sound Pathway to Pleasurable and Purposeful Reading

Margaret Perkins and Prue Goodwin

There are decades of research into how we read, how children learn to read and how best to teach it. Anyone training to be a teacher can find shelves of books in university libraries about the complex combination of skills and experiences involved in being a reader. Each book may offer slightly different advice; some authors may make bold statements about the efficacy of one teaching method or another, but all the authors will have set out with the genuine intention of enhancing learning experiences for children and improving general 'standards' of reading in society. Other sources of guidance available to teachers include government generated documents (for example, *The National Curriculum*, DfES/QCA, 2000; *NLS Framework for Teaching*, DfEE, 1998a), advice published by interested parties, such as librarians (The Reading Agency, 2004 *Enjoying Reading*) and many strongly worded articles and reports in journals and newspapers. Once qualified, however, it doesn't take long for most primary teachers to realize that, though very helpful, all the advice on offer cannot take into account the diverse range of needs within a class of up to 30 young children. For example, just one aspect of reading – learning to interpret the alphabetic code into meaning – has generated many different approaches from which to choose. As no one teaching method will be successful for every child, the rational teacher will look for and use whatever is helpful.

There is no doubt that for beginner readers a main element of learning to read is the process of making sense of written language as a symbol. If children are to become independent readers, they need to know how the symbolic system works and they need to be able to use and manipulate the 'code'. This is the aspect of reading referred to as 'phonics', and it involves learning the relationship between the speech sounds (phonemes) and their symbolic representation in the form of one or more letters of the alphabet (graphemes). It sounds surprisingly simple, yet it causes more debate among teachers, academics and politicians than any other aspect of the reading curriculum. It is essential that teachers understand how to navigate the debates, acquire a confident knowledge of literacy learning and provide pupils with positive learning experiences.

Typical classroom experiences

So what can we expect to see happening in a classroom run by a knowledgeable, confident and thoughtful teacher? There will be several different elements:

- an emphasis on hearing and distinguishing sounds;
- learning the relationship between the written symbol and sound;
- identifying common representations of sound and less usual ones;
- looking for patterns; and
- playing about with patterns.

All these activities will happen in different ways: they may be planned lessons with the whole class or a group; they may be incidental conversations about print during shared or guided reading or writing; they may be independent activities when children analyse and make words from letters by manipulating letters and letter combinations; they may be casual conversations about how print works or they may be opportunities to highlight print features in display and resources available to the children. All these different types of activities will be part of the teacher's planning so that lots of ways of using and talking about print are part of the children's classroom experience.

The first thing that children need to be able to do when tackling phonics is to hear and discriminate between the sounds. It is important that this is done before any explicit reference to how they are represented in print. The starting point is work on phonological awareness, that is, the ability to hear differences in speech sounds. Classroom activity related to phonological awareness will involve a lot of drama, movement, singing, clapping, listening and music:

- Singing songs and nursery rhymes that accentuate sound patterns (for example, *Hickory, Dickory Dock* and *Humpty Dumpty*), which help children 'tune' in to speech sounds.
- Sharing books with lots of opportunities to join in, especially with exciting noises such as those made by the dogs in *Yip Yap Snap!* (Fuge, 2001) or the traffic in *Noisy Noises On the Road* (Wells, 1988).
- Playing skipping and clapping games, which encourage rhythmic movement accompanied by words.
- Talking about the sounds we hear around us every day. Asking questions such as 'What sound does the cow make?', 'Can you hear the bell ring?' and 'Are you listening to the music?', all of which introduce very young children to the vocabulary of sound and encourage them to talk about the quality of sounds. 'That is a high sound.' 'That bell is ringing quickly.' 'That music makes me feel happy.'
- Listening to sounds and identifying and differentiating between those they hear. As they become more experienced, children will become more adept at hearing subtle differences between sounds.

All these activities become reading lessons as the children learn to hear, identify and discriminate between different sounds. In a classroom there would be lots of opportunities for children to play with sounds – a tape recorder, a sound area with materials to make sounds, displays of words to do with sounds. There would also be a specific focus on listening to sounds – group activities where sound lotto is played, making sound accompaniments to well-known stories, matching sounds with the objects or people who make them, trying to make different qualities of sound with voices and instruments.

Phonological awareness needs to be firmly established before moving to the next stage when children start to explore how sounds are represented in print. The purpose of our teaching is to enable children to become independent and effective readers, in control of written language. Although all the different sounds and their symbols must be learned, the whole experience should be firmly embedded in the complete meaning-making process. We may choose to make use of a published scheme (there is no point in reinventing the wheel) but, as schemes tend to adhere to one approach, we must avoid allowing it to dictate exclusively what happens in the class. Matching phoneme to grapheme is only one way that children will acquire the decoding skill. It is helpful to consider onset and rime, letter clusters and syllables. It is also important to look at words in their meaningful context, whether thinking about writing your own name or seeing a well-known story in print. Again there will be lots of activity in the room as letters and sounds are painted, sung, drawn in the sand, made by stretching arms and legs, spotted in displays around the school and even grown with cress seeds on bits of felt.

Of course, all the time that this focused work is going on, there will be plenty of other literacy experiences taking place. Everything related to literacy should be perceived by the children as interrelated. They need to be aware that working hard to remember a piece of grapho-phonic information holds the key to being able to read the super story book they shared yesterday.

Language and literacy-rich classrooms

A language-and literacy-rich classroom can be deceptive. It may look disorganized and unsystematic but the bedrock which underpins the excitement and activity is well-planned, systematic teaching. Every encounter with print will be planned to allow children to learn about both the nature and the function of written language. The purpose of phonic teaching is to enable independent access to the meaning of the text, and that must remain at the forefront of our thinking and planning.

Sound understanding is the aim, so we must take care how we talk about phonics. Sounds are represented by the symbols; the letters do not 'say' anything themselves. Children can become very confused by our careless use of language and we must be careful that we do not try to over-simplify and so be less accurate. We must remember that:

- There are no absolute rules in phonics. There are more common ways of representing sounds, but often well-known words do not conform to usual patterns. Think of the phoneme /ie/. It can be represented in many different ways: light, tie, eye, kite, I, climb, height, fly. Which is the most common? Which is the most unusual? Collecting words and sorting them is a powerful way of helping children to understand how the English language uses symbols to represent sound.

- Children need to understand that there are some differences which matter and some which don't. In their previous experience a chair has always been a chair, whichever way it is facing and whichever way up it is. Letters do not work like that. Playing with letters is a way of becoming familiar with their forms – magnetic letters, letters made from sandpaper, fur fabric, satin, wood, letters written on a partner's back, letter shapes I can make with my body, letters drawn in wet sand, in rice, in sawdust, letters painted in water on the playground, grown in cress on blotting paper, made out of play-dough. It is important to give children every possible opportunity of becoming familiar with the shapes of letters. Classrooms will be full of examples of written language which draw attention to letters representing sound. Alphabet charts can be made about almost every subject, letters can be highlighted in any print, words sharing a common rime can be listed, words with similar letter strings can be linked. Children's names can be used to explore the sound–symbol relationship.

- Listening to sounds and playing with them does not stop when we move to more focused phonic teaching. This too should be text based, and there are many wonderful books which play with language. Phonics is great fun when we find the rhymes in books like *The Cat in the Hat* by Dr Seuss, a *Preston Pig* story by Colin MacNaughton or the brilliant *Tanka Tanka Skunk* by Steve Webb.

- There are also some stories for young children beautifully written in lyric prose. The work of Martin Waddell, in particular, uses alliteration, assonance and rhyme as a natural part of his style. When children listen to *Farmer Duck* or *Can't you Sleep, Little Bear?* they are hearing and seeing literary language at its best.

There are many packages that offer good ideas for games that we can use with children or adapt for the special circumstances of the class. For example, the Primary National Strategy publication *Playing with Sounds* (DfES, 2003a) is an excellent resource, full of good ideas for exploring language in an enjoyable way. It contains examples of both child-initiated learning and play and planned teacher-directed activities.

Shared writing will be another way in which children will be taught explicitly how sounds are represented in print. Here it is the language of the teacher which will make that clear: 'How do I write down that word? It sounds like that other word we already know.' It is in situations like this that children come to realize that the same phoneme is not always represented in the same way; by exploring patterns they will come to appreciate both the conventions and the vagaries of English spelling, determined by morphemic structure (meaning, for example, 'sign' and 'signature') as well as phonological structure (sound).

The key characteristic of all these activities is that the alphabetic nature of written language is explored and taught within the context of texts which are meaningful and relevant to the children. Decoding is a means to an end and not an end in itself; once we know what a word 'says', we need to talk about what it means to us – how the story relates to our own feelings and experiences or how the text entertains, instructs, persuades or informs us. Readers and writers need phonic knowledge in order to engage with texts. It becomes one of the tools they use; struggling readers are often those who become stuck in the skill of using the tool rather than allowing the purpose of the literacy activity to dominate.

Although teaching should be logically organized, we must remember that learning is recursive – it spirals forwards in an irregular fashion rather than taking uniform steps along a straight line. It is not possible to say how or when every child will make a leap of understanding or which of the phonics-focused sessions prompted it. Synthetic phonics, analytic phonics, whole-to-part, onset and rime, analogy – all are available to teachers and all have their part to play in the early years classroom. In acknowledging different learning styles within the classroom, we can take every opportunity available to us. It will be when a young reader becomes lost in a book that everything falls into place. Above all, children need to enjoy reading and to share their personal responses to the variety of texts they encounter both in and out of the classroom. Acquiring phonic knowledge is just one of the essential steps to achieving that end.

A Commentary on this Classroom, by the Editors

Again you will have recognized similarities between some of the approaches mentioned in this account and in the two previous accounts in terms of the kinds of activities undertaken. This account, however, embeds the teaching of phonics within what is broadly called a 'whole language' approach. Emphasis is placed on understanding the purpose of reading and in reading enjoyable 'real books' – although the authors acknowledge the usefulness of reading schemes too. Knowledge about language is discussed and language is seen as a flexible and intriguing tool rather than a set of unbreakable rules. Phonic rules are given attention but are not an end in themselves. The personal and social aspects of language learning are invoked and a literacy-rich physical and social environment central to the quality of learning. The role of the teacher is characterized as that of a skilled practitioner orchestrating many aspects of language learning, not merely as a deliverer of programmes. Pace and content are more personalized to the needs of the learner.

SOMETHING TO THINK ABOUT

- In Chapter 1, Kathy Hall argues that different views about the role of phonics reflect deeper differences about how we view knowledge. What different views of knowledge do you think are represented in these three classrooms?

SOMETHING TO READ

- The nine papers from the government's phonics seminar held in 2003 include submissions from those who advocate a purely synthetic approach, an NLS approach and an approach that places greater emphasis on meaning. You can select from these papers if you wish to explore any of these approaches in greater detail, available online at www.standards.dfes.gov.uk/primary/publications/literacy/686807/

SOMETHING TO DO

- With colleagues, read through each of the teachers' accounts and compile a list of all the classroom practices that seem important. Discuss which practices are absolutely central to your own practice, which are present but not particularly high-profile, and which are not part of your current classroom practice. Are there any aspects that you think might be worth further investigation?
- What do you think each of these teachers would say about how you teach phonics to your own class? If they had to suggest one thing that you should change, what do you think it would be, and why? Discuss these suggestions with colleagues and consider which might be worth trying.

Chapter 5

Involving Parents and Carers

Jackie Marsh

The importance of teaching children to hear, identify and manipulate language, that is developing their phonological and phonemic awareness, has been well established by research (Byrant and Bradley, 1985; Maclean et al., 1987; NRP, 2000a). There is also widespread evidence that children's early reading development can be fostered by parents* and carers (Hannon, 2003; Nutbrown et al., 2005) and, in this chapter, approaches to involving parents in this work will be reviewed.

The chapter focuses on the development of phonological and phonemic awareness, but that does not mean that work with parents should concentrate on this area to the exclusion of others. Indeed, it is important that parents develop a balanced approach to fostering their children's reading progress, as an over-emphasis on aspects such as the ability to recognize and manipulate phonemes can be counter-productive. However, given that the emphasis of this book is on the teaching and learning of phonics, this chapter offers guidance to teachers on possible approaches that could be made. In addition, focusing on the role of parents should not exclude schools from considering the involvement of wider family members in literacy programmes and workshops, given that research has indicated that grandparents, aunts, uncles and siblings, for example, can all play important roles in children's reading development (Gregory et al., 2004).

Before strategies that can be used to involve parents are considered, it is important to remember that both phonological awareness and phonemic awareness in spoken language are key precursors to attainment in phonics. Therefore, in the early stages of reading, children need plenty of opportunities

---

*Throughout the chapter, the word 'parents' is used to refer to both biological and non-biological parents and carers.

to hear and play with sounds aurally. Teachers need to stress this to parents as, often, parents move straight to work on phoneme-grapheme correspondence when this is developmentally inappropriate for their children.

There are a number of approaches to involving parents in children's early reading. At the simplest level, teachers can engage parents in one-to-one conversations about how they can support reading, and perhaps use parent-friendly literature that can be taken home and used when parents need additional guidance. An alternative is to offer specially designed one-off workshops that introduce parents to key strategies. Holding regular drop-in sessions for parents is also helpful and allows them to return to issues if they find they need extra support. Finally, a series of workshops can be organized as part of a structured family literacy programme. Whatever approach is used, it is important for schools to be clear about how they will involve parents in early reading and to communicate this to families. Simply sending books home for parents to share with children will not always lead to best practice. When considering setting up a programme (however informal) for parents, a number of principles should be considered.

Key principles that should underpin work with parents

The following section offers a set of guiding principles that could inform work with parents, but is not an exhaustive list; schools will want to add principles arising from a consideration of their own specific contexts.

Respecting and building on home practices

Many of the approaches taken to developing parental engagement in literacy in the past have been predicated on schooled notions of what it means to be an engaged parent, notions which are often conflated with the socio-cultural practices of white, middle-class families (Carrington and Luke, 2003). In some family literacy programmes, ideas, concepts and best practice have been introduced in ways which have masked the already rich range of practices that parents and carers are engaged in at home. Rather than imposing a given set of practices upon parent groups, the approaches in this chapter are based on the principle that a starting point for any work with parents should be a recognition of the 'funds of knowledge' (Moll et al., 1992) that they bring with them to the task of helping their children to learn to read. If possible, it is always useful to begin family literacy work with a survey of what is already happening in the home so that future work can acknowledge and build upon this. It is also helpful to let parents have a voice in the content and structure of programmes in order that they meet the needs of families.

The primacy of oracy

In any work with parents to support early reading development, there should be a key emphasis on parents fostering children's oral language. Nutbrown et al. point out that 'Three aspects of oral language appear to be key to children's literacy learning and development: storytelling, phonological awareness and talk about literacy' (1995: 47). This chapter focuses on the second of these, but parents and teachers should also be aware of the other important elements of oracy.

The importance of pleasure

Parents need to recognize that any activities they undertake with their children should be occasions that are pleasurable and fun for all concerned. Placing pressure on children to achieve specific skills could lead to children becoming stressed and adopting a negative attitude to reading. Many of the approaches to developing phonemic awareness that are mentioned in this chapter are inherently pleasurable and can be embedded in a range of everyday activities, such as having fun with word strings and rhymes on bus and car journeys, signing along with jingles when watching adverts and favourite videos and playing with alliteration and assonance linked to family names ('Eddie eats every egg', 'Herat sat in a flat').

The balanced approach

As suggested in the opening to this chapter, parents need to understand that beginning reading requires the child to orchestrate a number of different cues and any input to promote reading development needs to maintain a balance between work on whole texts, words and individual phonemes. The emphasis needs to be placed on meaningful engagement with print. In particular, storybook reading has been identified as a key element of early literacy experiences in the home. Storybook reading enhances children's attitudes to reading (Baker et al., 1997; Baker et al., 2001) as well as their concepts of print, receptive language development, vocabulary and comprehension skills (Sénéchal and Lefevre, 2002). Storybook reading in itself is not the main factor in success; it is the *quality* of the interaction between the adult and the child during storybook reading that is important (Sénéchal and Lefevre, 2002). More effective parental practice includes drawing children's attention to letters and words, asking them to predict events and prompting children to reflect beyond a literal interpretation of the text (Sénéchal and Lefevre, 2002; Whitehurst et al., 1998). It is important that the reading experience is enjoyable for the child. Baker et al. (1997) found that increased enjoyment of reading was related to discussions about the stories with parents and that this impacted positively on motivation for reading in school.

In addition to storybook reading, other aspects of parental involvement in early literacy are important for reading development. Parental attitudes towards literacy, number of books owned, wider provision of literacy resources in the home, library membership and educational aspirations for the child all predict levels of emergent literacy skills (Purcell-Gates, 1996; Raz and Bryant, 1990; Share et al., 1984; White, 1982). A range of activities is most beneficial and preferable to any single interaction between parents and children (Sénéchal and Lefevre, 2002). These issues could be discussed with parents in order to raise their awareness of the need for a broad and balanced approach to the development of reading.

Active engagement

Workshops for parents should provide plenty of opportunities for parents to try out activities and to rehearse the strategies that are introduced to them. This can develop parents' confidence and enhance their self-esteem.

Once fundamental approaches to working with parents have been established by schools, teachers can set about designing workshops and programmes that will provide parents with guidance on supporting children's early reading development. If it is not possible to hold such sessions, then teachers should at least attempt to engage parents in regular conversations about supporting children's reading, providing them with strategies and guidance where necessary through handouts and lists of websites. However, research shows that family literacy programmes are effective (Hannon, 2003; Nutbrown et al., 2005) and, where possible, schools should strive to engage parents in structured sessions that offer opportunities to build confidence and skills.

The following section considers ways that parents can be encouraged to support children's reading.

How to promote engagement

There are numerous books with ideas for games and activities with children that parents can use to promote children's engagement in early reading. Such activities need an underpinning framework to help parents gain a broader picture of where the activities fit in children's overall reading experiences. The ORIM Framework is a model that has worked for a number of schools and Local Authorities and is used by the Raising Early Achievement in Literacy (REAL) Project (Nutbrown et al., 2005). The framework identifies four strands of early literacy development: environmental print, books, early writing and key aspects of oral language. It also outlines four key roles for parents in which they can provide: Opportunities, Recognition, Interaction and a Model of literacy in each of the four early literacy strands. Table 5.1 provides further details of these key roles and what each of them entails.

Opportunities	• Materials for promoting oracy, reading and writing. • Encouraging play. • Providing opportunities for interactions with print, e.g. noticing environmental print on shopping trips.
Recognition	• Identifying early milestones in children's development. • Displaying children's drawings and writing. • Providing praise and feedback to children on achievements.
Interaction	• Making the most of opportunities to interact with children in oracy, reading and writing activities, e.g. when writing to family members, reading the television guide. • Showing children how to undertake certain tasks. • Playing with children.
Model	• Acting as role models for children by drawing attention to the way in which parents use literacy in everyday life, e.g. reading newspapers, completing forms.

Table 5.1   Four key roles for parents (Nutbrown et al., 2005)

This model offers a useful structure for promoting parents' involvement in children's early reading development. As this chapter is focused on the development of phonological and phonemic awareness, Table 5.2 provides an example of how the ORIM Framework might be used to outline possible approaches that can be made by parents in fostering this area of reading development.

This framework can then be applied to other strands of early literacy development to support work with parents (see Nutbrown et al., 2005 for numerous examples of such work). As suggested previously, there are many more ways in which parents can promote phonological, phonemic awareness and phonics than the approaches outlined in Table 5.2, but the key emphasis should be on activities which are fun, easy for parents to grasp and related to everyday practices. To read further suggestions for such activities, see Bayley and Broadbent (2005), who offer a wealth of ideas.

There are also now many websites for parents that offer guidance and resources for supporting children's early reading development. However, some of these sites do promote an overuse of worksheets that can be printed off for children to complete. Teachers should emphasize that parents need to be careful when accessing websites and should choose sites that offer fun, interactive games and activities that embed positive feedback within them. Often, newly-released popular films have related websites that include good-quality games and these can be highly motivating for children. Using children's popular culture in early literacy work can orientate children to tasks and enhance engagement (Marsh, in

	Activities to promote phonological awareness	Activities to promote phonemic awareness/phonics
Opportunities	• Borrow nursery rhyme books from the local library. • Make a tape of favourite nursery rhymes (or a podcast if parents are up-to-date with technology!). • Raise parents' awareness of opportunities to identify rhymes in the environment, e.g. adverts, jingles.	• Raise parents' awareness of the opportunities for engagement with print in the home environment, e.g. junk mail. • Borrow alphabet books from the local library. • Buy a set of magnetic letters for the fridge. • Talk about opportunities for promoting engagement with print on visits and walks.
Recognition	• Parents should be informed about the ways in which they can recognize children's developing phonological awareness, e.g. being able to clap syllables in names; awareness of onset–rime.	• Parents should be informed about the ways in which they can recognize children's developing phonemic awareness, e.g. being able to identify individual phonemes in words. Stress that this needs to be done orally before children match phonemes to graphemes.
Interaction	• Clap out the syllables in names and other familiar words. • Re-tell nursery rhymes, omitting the final rhyming word for the child to supply, e.g. 'Humpty Dumpty sat on a wall, Humpty Dumpty had a great __'. • Make a scrapbook of favourite nursery rhymes, using pictures from magazines and catalogues to portray the characters/events.	• When encountering street signs, say the words out loud and encourage children to identify beginning, middle and end phonemes, e.g. shop – sh/o/p. • Ask children to provide the last phoneme in a word after offering them a clue to the word, e.g. 'It is something you read, it's a boo_'. • Collect together items which begin with the same sound and place them in a bag. Emphasize the initial sound as you say the word when the child takes the item out of the bag.

Table 5.2 Using the ORIM Framework for work on phonological and phonemic awareness and phonics (Nutbrown et al., 2005)

	Activities to promote phonological awareness	Activities to promote phonemic awareness/phonics
Interaction (continued)	• Make up rhyming sentences that relate to children's favourite television and film characters, e.g. 'Postman Pat has a dark blue hat'. • Place rhyming objects in a bag and repeat the rhyming words with children as you take them out, e.g. clock, sock, lock, rock. • Ask child to think of as many words as he/she can that end with the same rime, e.g. can, pan, man, fan.	• Make a popular cultural alphabet book. Using a scrapbook or file of individual blank sheets, cut out pictures of favourite television characters or use photographs from catalogues, sweet wrappers and so on. Stick these on the relevant pages, e.g. the 'M' page might contain a picture of Milo from the Tweenies and a wrapper from a Mars Bar.
Model	• Draw children's attention to occasions when parents sing rhymes and jingles, e.g. 'You can do it when you B&Q it!'	• Parents can talk about individual sounds in words as they write lists, complete crosswords.

Table 5.2 (Continued)

press). Parents also need guidance on the very wide range of materials that are now on offer in supermarkets and bookshops to support early learning. Again, some of these contain developmentally and pedagogically inappropriate material. Developing a set of criteria for choosing such material could usefully be an activity included in a family literacy workshop.

Working with bilingual families

For schools that serve multilingual communities, working with parents provides a range of opportunities, but also additional challenges. Not all parents may be able to speak English and some may not be literate in either English or their first language. However, much can be done in work with families on early reading development, as the following case study of Springfield School, Sheffield, indicates. Here, the Deputy Headteacher, Val Johnson, outlines some approaches the school has taken to work with parents on reading:

Springfield Primary School, Sheffield

Most of our parents are bilingual and many do not read or write English and so we can't just send home reading books with children and expect parents to share them with their children. Nor are the reading record books that many schools send home with children for parents to write in appropriate for our families. So we have done a number of things to develop parents' engagement with their children's learning. We have held workshops with translators in which we have had a few parents at a time attend, as that allows intensive work. We emphasize that it is important for parents to talk to children at home using their first language. We spend a lot of time talking about how they can support their child through sharing stories, talking about books using the pictures and taking an interest in what they do. We have also had a storysacks project in which parents made bilingual storysacks. This gives parents the message that we value their home languages and also increases confidence in re-telling stories that they are familiar with. We also use photographs of trips that parents have been on with children to make books – these shared events can provide a good opportunity for talk around texts.

Other strategies that can be used to involve bilingual parents in early reading development include:

- Making a video for parents in their first language which explains how children develop reading skills and how they can help them, even if parents are not able to read English, for example, by talking about the pictures, re-telling the story through the pictures.
- Helping parents to make tapes of rhymes and stories in the children's first language.
- Giving parents digital or disposable cameras and asking them to take photographs of everyday objects at home. These can then be used to make dual-language alphabet books to share with their children. Collective approaches to some of the more challenging letters (for example, x and z) can be taken!

Another group of parents that can often be difficult to reach is fathers. It is primarily mothers who attend family literacy programmes, even in schools in which a significant proportion of parents who bring children to school are men. This may reflect the gendered patterns with regard to literacy, in that research has indicated that many women read more often at home than men and are more involved in literacy activities with their children (Millard, 1996). But there are strategies that can be used to encourage men to take part in activities that promote early reading and these are outlined in the next section.

Working with fathers

In the following case study, Gary Roberts and the Aberdeen Family Learning Team outline how men were targeted for involvement in family learning programmes. The projects were funded by Learning Connections, the Adult Literacy section of Community Scotland.

CASE STUDY

Challenge Dad Pathfinder Project, Aberdeen

We have done a lot of work to involve fathers in children's early literacy development. In conversations with fathers, we found that many of them wanted to be involved with children's literacy development but didn't know what to do, they felt excluded. Many of the fathers we worked with were football fans and felt comfortable around football grounds. So we organized trips in which fathers and sons visited the grounds together and noted down the environmental print as they went around, talking about the beginning letters of words and playing games like 'I spy'. The fathers and their children also made books about the visit. We used disposable cameras and the dads and sons and daughters took photographs. They chose the pictures that they wanted to go in the books and discussed the literacy practices in them. It's amazing how much print they found, on football scarves and T-shirts and things like that. It was a great success in that the fathers felt much more confident about supporting children's reading development and the children loved the involvement of their dads.

Other strategies to involve fathers in early reading development include:

- Creating a home–school comic-lending library: previous projects have shown that fathers have enjoyed sharing comics with children (Millard and Marsh, 2003).
- Asking dads to make books about their interests and hobbies for their children: for example, a dad in one school made a book about fishing for his son using photographs and pictures from fishing magazines. The

school staff helped him to use language appropriate for beginning readers, and his son loved reading a book that his own dad had made.

- Dads' favourite books: one school used a wall in a corridor to document the favourite books of children's fathers, displaying copies of book covers where possible, along with speech bubbles containing the fathers' thoughts on the books they had named as favourites.
- Setting up a *Curiosity Kits* scheme: non-fiction book bags with related artefacts that have been shown to encourage book sharing between children and males in the family (Lewis and Fisher, 2003).

There are a number of potentially sensitive areas in this work. Some children may live in single-parent families and not be in regular contact with their fathers. Focusing on fathers' involvement may cause distress to some children in these cases. It is also important that any attempts to involve fathers do not draw energies away from developing family learning more generally. Both mothers and fathers need to feel welcomed in school and able to become involved in family learning projects. Balancing all of these elements in any work with families is never easy, but is important in order to ensure widespread involvement.

Conclusion

This chapter has explored a number of approaches to involving parents in children's early reading development. The key emphasis has been on fostering parents' awareness of how they can develop children's phonological and phonemic awareness in fun and exciting ways. It is important that parents realize that work on phonemic awareness does not have to be planned for as a discrete activity, but can be woven into the fabric of everyday life.

Whatever approaches you take to working with parents in your school, it will be important to monitor and review them. There will, inevitably, be some approaches that are more effective than others, for a variety of reasons. Documenting responses can enable you to evaluate the various strategies and to develop further the most successful ones. In addition, engaging in such work year after year will enable you to build up a strong stock of resources and approaches, which can include the parents themselves. For example, you could involve some of the parents who have undertaken workshops in guiding and mentoring new parents, who may feel unsure about how to help their children. These 'parent buddies' can be invaluable in supporting the work that you do. Above all, it is important to remember that teachers cannot and should not undertake the task of educating children alone. Partnerships with parents are key to children's educational achievement (Desforges and Abouchaar, 2003), and some of the early work teachers and parents do to support children's early literacy development is crucial to the fostering of strong partnerships that will last. This chapter can only offer a few glimpses into this significant area of work and so is followed by some suggestions for further activities and reading.

SOMETHING TO THINK ABOUT

- What could you do to promote parents' engagement in their children's early reading development that you are not currently doing? For example, could you recruit 'parent buddies' to support new parents?
- What extra resources do you need in order to develop these new activities? Are you making the most of the parents themselves? Parents of older children in school might be only too willing to donate to parents of younger children reading games and resources that their children have grown out of.
- How can you include those hard-to-reach families and fathers in this work?

SOMETHING TO READ

- Bayley, R. and Broadbent, L. (2005) *Flying Start with Literacy: Activities for parents and children.* Stafford: Network Educational Press. This book offers a wide range of suggestions for activities that parents can undertake with children, with an emphasis on fun and active engagement.
- Gregory, E., Long, S. and Volk, D. (2004) *Many Pathways to Literacy.* London: RoutledgeFalmer. This book provides a number of rich case studies which outline how bilingual families support children's literacy development. The emphasis is on the engagement of wider family members, such as siblings, grandparents, aunts and uncles, not just parents.
- Nutbrown, C., Hannon, P. and Morgan, A. (2005) *Early Literacy Work with Families: Policy, practice and research.* London: Sage. This book outlines the REAL Project and provides detailed guidance on using the ORIM Framework with families.

SOMETHING TO DO

- Conduct a survey of current reading practice in the homes of the children you teach in order to inform parental development work in your school.
- Refer parents to the helpful CBeebies website which contains articles on how children learn, including a section on language and literacy: www.bbc.co.uk/cbeebies/grownups/
- Visit the National Literacy Trust's website in order to find out about other parental programmes in the United Kingdom: www.literacy trust.org.uk

Chapter 6

Developmental Issues: Speaking and Phonological Awareness

Elspeth McCartney

By the time that normally developing children begin to learn to read and write they have already learned to talk. This means that they have succeeded in segmenting the stream of sound they hear into meaningful words, and learned how to pronounce most of the words of English. Learning to relate written forms such as words and letters to their auditory counterpart continues a process that started in infancy.

Learning to talk involves recognizing, representing and storing the phonemes (speech sounds) of the languages heard by a child. Each word in a language has its own phonological form, stored alongside the word's meanings in the lexicon (mental word store). Identifying a word spoken by another or saying it aloud requires that the correct phonological form is identified or used. Long before they learn to read or write, children analyse the phonemes of the language(s) to which they are exposed, but do this on a largely unconscious level. By the time they learn to decode written text they have created an internal template of the language's phonemes and word forms and can match written words against this, as a step in accessing meaning. This chapter traces children's development of phonological representations and their growing ability to reflect upon them consciously, and considers some of the implications of this process for learning to read. It begins with a brief overview of the phonology of English to clarify the information that children bring to the process of reading.

The phonology of English

The English language uses about 40 distinct elements to form all the words of the language (and English may have about half a million words). These elements are called 'phonemes'. Phonemes are divided into vowels and consonants and contrast the words of a language so that changing a phoneme can change the meaning. Think of words like 'c̲at', 'b̲at', 'f̲at', 'r̲at', 's̲at', 'p̲at', 't̲at', 'v̲at', 'c̲hat', 't̲hat', 'h̲at', which differ only in their initial phoneme. Understanding how phonemes are formed can help to explain why young children confuse phonemes that adults may feel are 'obviously' different. Often the confused phonemes are quite close in articulatory terms.

Vowels

Vowels and consonants are most easily defined by considering how a speaker's breath is shaped in the mouth as it passes from the lungs whilst talking. For vowel sounds the breath is not stopped or occluded on the way, although every vowel has a 'buzz' of voicing added from the vocal cords vibrating together in the larynx (also called the voice box or Adam's apple). The air passes out fairly freely, shaped only a little by the tongue and lips.

To make different vowels, we need to think about the physical positions adopted by the tongue and lips and how close the tongue is held to the roof of the mouth. The back or front of the tongue can be bunched up more or less closely to the roof of the mouth, or the tongue can be held fairly flat; the lips can be rounded or spread. To understand the very tiny differences that children must notice, try this sequence: round your lips, and hold the tip of your tongue down behind your lower teeth. This leaves the tongue bunched up high at the back and lets you make 'back' vowels. Make a 'high' to 'low' vowel sequence (start with the back of the tongue close to the roof of your mouth) whilst letting some air out and sounding at the larynx. You should first get an 'oo' vowel, as in 'oodles'. Lower the back of the tongue to make 'oh', as in 'over'; then lower it further to 'o' as in 'orange' then 'ah' as in 'bath'. Now make 'front' vowels, with the front of your tongue bunched up near the roof of your mouth with lips spread, giving 'ee' as in 'eerie', then lower your tongue a little for 'eh' as in 'empty' and lower it further for 'a' as in 'apple'. There are also vowels made with the centre of the tongue ('central' vowels) like the 'u' in 'utter', the 'i' in 'insect' and the 'e' in 'the'. Many unstressed syllables in English words use this last vowel sound, although spelled in all sorts of ways. To make things even more complicated for children, vowels can follow each other very rapidly in a word, forming 'diphthongs'. Say 'a' with 'ee' to make the vowel sound in 'my'; 'a' with 'oo' to make the vowel sound in 'now', and 'o' with 'i' to make the vowel sound 'boy'. There are great differences among the accents of English in the exact sound of vowels heard, and considerable variation within and across speakers.

Consonants

The consonants of English (see Table 6.1) are also classified by the mouth movements used to realize them. Consonants can be either voiced or voiceless – compare these by putting a finger and thumb tip on either side of your larynx, and saying 'f' followed by 'v', or 's' followed by 'z'. You should feel the voicing 'buzz' on the 'v' and 'z' sounds, which are 'voiced' consonants, but not on the 'f' or 's', where the air passes through the larynx without the vocal cords vibrating, making 'voiceless' sounds.

Consonants are also defined by whether the air-stream coming through the lungs is completely stopped for a short time in the mouth then released with a small explosive noise (called 'stop' or 'plosive' consonants); squeezed between two parts of the mouth moving close together (making 'fricative' and 'glide' consonants); or released through the nose rather than the mouth. These features are called the 'manner' of release. In voiced and voiceless pairs the 'stop' or 'plosive' consonants (both terms are used) are 'p', 'b'; 't', 'd'; and 'k', 'g'. When children confuse 'p' and 'b' or 't' and 'd', we need to remember that it is a tiny difference (approximately 40 milliseconds of vocal cord vibration) that distinguishes them. The 'fricatives' are 'f', 'v'; 's', 'z'; 'sh', 'zh'; 'th' both voiced and voiceless and 'h', where two parts of the mouth come so close together that we hear the turbulence as the sound is squeezed through.

The 'affricates' have air stopped as for a 't' or 'd' but released as for a fricative 'sh' or 'zh', giving the voiced and voiceless affricates 'ch' as in 'chur_ch_' (from 't + sh') and 'j' as in 'jury' (from 'd + zh'). The last group of consonants released through the mouth are the glides 'l' as in '_l_ook'; 'r' as in '_r_ed'; 'w' as in '_w_et'; and 'y' as in '_y_ellow'. The air passes through the mouth more freely than for stops, fricatives or affricates, but less freely than for vowels.

There are also three voiced consonants, 'm', 'n' and 'ng' as in 'ri_ng_' where the air-stream is released through the nose, and is blocked off from the mouth for their short duration by the soft palate (back of the roof of the mouth) rising up. Say these three sounds with a thumb and finger either side of your nose, and feel the sound resonating there. Then hold a small mirror just under your nose as you say them – you will see it mist up, as the air comes through. The nasal sounds 'm' and 'n' are heard early in children's speech.

The last way in which consonants are classified is by the place they are made in the mouth. The two parts of the mouth that meet together or come close together in English can be the two lips; the top teeth and lower lip; the tongue tip and back of the top teeth, the tongue tip and hard palate (roof of the mouth), or the tongue back and the soft palate (velum). The larynx itself can shape the air just enough so that 'h' is heard. The figure below gives the consonant sounds of English classified as above, including the bilabial and velar fricatives heard in Scottish English in '_wh_ite' and 'lo_ch_'.

Some of these consonants may look unfamiliar as they do not have particular letters attached to them. English uses the grapheme 'th' for both the tongue–teeth fricatives (the voiceless 'th' as in '_th_ought' and voiced 'th' as in '_th_ough'). The voiced version is heard at the start of closed-class words like '_th_e', '_th_en', '_th_ou' and '_th_at' whereas the voiceless consonant can start content words like nouns ('_th_umb', '_th_atcher', '_th_imble'), verbs ('_th_ink', '_th_ump') and adjectives ('_th_orough', '_th_in'). Adults may not notice that there are two

Place in mouth	Manner of release (Voiced consonants are in bold)				
	Stops	Nasals	Fricatives	Affricates	Glides
Two lips	p, **b**	**m**	wh		**w**
Lip and teeth			f, **v**		
Tongue and teeth			th, **th**		
Tongue tip and gum ridge	t, **d**	**n**	s, **z**		**l, r**
Body of tongue and hard palate			sh, **zh**	ch, **j**	**y**
Back of tongue and soft palate	k, **g**	**ng**	lo<u>ch</u>		
Larynx			h		

Table 6.1   The consonants of English (adapted from McCartney, 1984: 18)

phonemes because both are written as 'th', but the existence of two phonemes and one spelling can confuse children. Similarly the 'zh' phoneme that is only heard in the middle of words such as 'mea<u>s</u>ure', 'plea<u>s</u>ure' and 'trea<u>s</u>ure' and in 'borrowed' words like 'bei<u>ge</u>' and 'rou<u>ge</u>', <u>G</u>igi and <u>Zh</u>a<u>zh</u>a may not be noticed by adults.

As adults, we also unconsciously accept the rules governing how many consonants can appear in sequence at the start and end of English words: one, two or three at the start before a vowel is needed (so that '<u>str</u>ing' would be among the longest sequences permitted) and up to four at the end (as in 'scu<u>lpts</u>', where the grammar marker 's' gives four phonemes). We also know that only some consonants can follow others in clusters; try saying both the 'k' and 'n' at the start of 'knife', for an example of a cluster of consonants that has dropped out of English, or reversing the 'l' and 's' in 'slip' for a pattern that does not occur. Some consonants occur only in particular syllable positions, for example 'ng' appears at the end of syllables as in 'ri<u>ng</u>i<u>ng</u>' but not at the start.

There is variation in consonant use among speakers and among English accents: 'r' is not heard after a vowel in some accents, and voiceless 'th' is becoming 'f' in others, but less variation in consonants than among vowels.

For young children, the picture gets even more complicated when we think about connected speech rather than individual sounds. Speech is the most rapid motor sequence that humans undertake, and when we talk, the consonants are not realized in their full forms as classified above. The rapid movements required for speech mean that phonemes accommodate to the sounds around them. For example, consider the word 'have' in the sentence 'I must have been wrong', said at normal conversational rate (which is fast!). The word is unstressed in this sentence and its vowel sound will become rather central. The unvoiced consonant 'h' at the start follows two unvoiced consonants, the 's' and 't' cluster in 'mu<u>st</u>', and will tend not to be heard since voicing coming in for the vowel will mask it. A child writing 'I must have . . .' as 'I must of . . .' may be responding to such factors, playing the sentence through their internal phonological representations, and coming up with the very similar sounding word 'of' (which has a central vowel followed by phoneme 'v', although this is written 'f'). There is a tiny difference in sound, but resulting in a big mistake in writing.

Assimilation can also occur within words, for example across syllable boundaries. The rapid nature of speech means that speakers tend to collapse phonemes, moving mouth parts together for one but opening them for the next. An example is the word 'handbag', which is usually pronounced 'hambag'. Here the nasality from the phoneme 'n' is reflected in the nasal 'm', which has moved forward to the lip position required to open for 'b'. (Such features can occasionally become fixed in spelling: the county of Du<u>n</u>bartonshire in Scotland, from *Dun Briton*, fort of the Britons, contains the town Du<u>m</u>barton, where the spelling has changed to reflect the pronunciation.) Such assimilation is not due to 'lazy' or 'slovenly' speech, nor to particular accents, but is a universal accommodation to the limits of rapid muscle movement in humans. However, it can pose problems for children who arrive at literacy with an auditory-based system, and then meet the complexities of English spelling.

English phonology and spelling

The phonemes of English are represented highly inconsistently in written words, even common words – much more so than in languages such as Italian. This is partly because pronunciation has changed during the history of the language, and the written form preserves an earlier pronunciation. For example, certain words spelled with 'gh' reflect pronunciations still retained in some Scottish dialects, such as 'daughter' said with a velar fricative (as in Scottish 'lo<u>ch</u>') in the middle. Similarly, 'two' said as 'twa' is closer to the older pronunciations and the spelling than the standard English pronunciation 'too'. Other words have been imported directly from different languages with their spellings intact, such as 'role' as in 'role-play' from the French 'rôle'. Retaining spelling patterns close to the original helps readers distinguish among the many words in English with different meanings that sound exactly the same (here 'roll' which exists as a noun and a verb) and can help a reader to access the right meaning quickly. But spelling variations can cause difficulties for early readers and writers trying to map written forms to their internalized sound-based template of English phonology.

One of the most awkward features of English writing is in the spelling of vowels. For example, the vowel 'oh' as in 'over', which most people would agree was one vowel, can be represented as in 'b<u>ow</u>', 'd<u>ough</u>', 't<u>oe</u>', 'g<u>o</u>', 's<u>ew</u>', 'b<u>oat</u>', 'f<u>our</u>', 'b<u>one</u>', 'c<u>ourse</u>' and 'fl<u>oor</u>', where the letters underlined represent no phoneme except the vowel. Consonants also have variations: consonant 's', for example, can be written at the start of a syllable as in '<u>s</u>ee', '<u>sc</u>ience', 'p<u>s</u>ychology' or '<u>c</u>ycle' and at the end as in 'ga<u>s</u>' or 'me<u>ss</u>'. Its voiced twin 'z' can be as in '<u>z</u>ip', 'pi<u>zz</u>a' or '<u>s</u>cissors' at the start of a syllable, and as in 'ma<u>z</u>e', 'ja<u>zz</u>' or 'ha<u>s</u>' at the end. Consonant 'sh' can be as in '<u>sh</u>ip' or '<u>s</u>ugar'; 'f' as in '<u>f</u>ire' or '<u>ph</u>oto'; 'ch' as in '<u>ch</u>ur<u>ch</u>' or 'wa<u>tch</u>', and 'j' has two different spellings in the same word '<u>j</u>u<u>dg</u>e'. The letter 'x' often represents two phonemes, 'k' plus 's' or 'g' plus 'z' said as a cluster – for e<u>x</u>ample! Much of this has to be learned as word-specific spelling, and teachers spend time teaching rules, word 'families', analogies and sometimes the reasons for odd spellings to help children cope with the variations encountered. Chapter 8 gives further examples.

The development of phonology

Perception and categorization

Children learn to perceive and pronounce the speech sounds of their language(s) very early, utilizing biological and social constraints on communicative learning. Kuhl (2004) reviews the development of speech perception, and notes that infants from birth are highly sensitive to acoustic changes that distinguish phonemic boundaries important in many languages. They very rapidly learn categories specific to their own language(s), so that by about 12 months of age English-learning babies have difficulty in distinguishing phonemes that are not heard in English, and even at six months old can group vowels from their native language together in contrast to those of another language. Infants learn to detect common stress patterns of words, and 'legal' and 'illegal' phoneme combinations, based on their preference by nine months for phonetic patterns that occur frequently.

Speech

Learning the spoken forms of phonemes is affected by the development of motor skills. Whether because human children develop oral motor abilities in similar ways and at similar rates, or for some other reason, there is a predictable pattern in which phonemes are acquired across languages by little children. Vowel sounds appear early, and are often remarkably accurate. Broadly speaking, consonants made at the front of the mouth are heard early, then those made in the middle, then those at the back. In English this gives rise to the sequence 'p', 'b'; then 't', 'd'; with 'k', 'g' later. Fricatives are often realized by a stop sound made at a similar place in the mouth to the fricative, and glides are

9 months – 18 months:	Plosives and nasals. Within this group front consonants may replace back consonants; consonants at the start of words may be repeated in the middle of words; final consonants may be deleted; plosives replace fricatives and affricates.
18 months – 30 months:	Fricatives are added. They may not be used correctly until over five years.
36 months plus:	Affricates are added. They may not be used correctly until over five years.
Until five years:	'w' heard instead of 'l' and 'r'.
30 months – five years plus:	Consonant clusters, with 's' and 'r' clusters last.

The consonant system is usually complete by seven years.

Table 6.2 The age at which consonants are usually heard (adapted from McCartney, 1984: 18)

often assimilated to 'w'. Single consonants are heard before clusters, so that 'spoon' becomes 'poon', and unstressed syllables and final consonants are omitted – 'banana' becomes 'nana' and 'book' becomes 'boo'. A combination of these processes produces typical 'baby talk'. Processes also disappear at predictable times in child development, making it possible to determine if a child is progressing normally or showing delay in speech development. Dodd et al. (2005) give an overview of phonological acquisition. The ages at which consonants are typically used is outlined in Table 6.2.

As Table 6.2 shows, many children begin learning to read before they show complete mastery of the consonant system of English. They can, however, gain from phonological approaches to reading; indeed, many speech and language therapists also use activities that develop phonological awareness to help children with speech delay to develop their speech. In general, children with early speech problems have normal internal representations of the phonology of English and learn to read and spell successfully (Snowling et al., 2000), although children with persisting impairments in other aspects of language such as grammar and word-learning often show significant literacy difficulties (Stothard et al., 1998).

Whilst not being able to pronounce a speech sound is not usually a reason for being unable to perceive it or to learn its varied spellings, there are a small number of children who use speech patterns that are uncommon in 'typically developing' children, such as 'backing' sounds to the velar position or omitting word initial consonants. Such children are often quite unintelligible. They are thought to have difficulty in building up internal phonological representations, and can as a group show long-term evidence of reading comprehension difficulties

(Leitão and Fletcher, 2004). These children may need help from speech and language therapists and learning support teachers. Any child using such unusual speech patterns should certainly set alarm bells ringing.

Children learn to perceive and use the phonology of English without being able to reflect consciously on the internal phonological representations they are developing. Our understanding of their abilities is gained through experimental tasks and analysing their speech output: they cannot tell us the rules they are developing, nor manipulate the phonology of words. As children approach the age of school entry, however, they become more consciously aware of phonology, and can be encouraged to think about speech sounds as identifiable elements. This conscious awareness and ability to manipulate phonology has been described as phonological awareness, and may be an important factor in predicting the ease with which children will map their (accurate) internal representations of the phonology of English on to its (imperfect) alphabetical system. See Chapter 8 for a detailed discussion of the orthography of English.

Phonological awareness

Phonological awareness is defined by Torgesen et al. as a 'sensitivity to, or explicit awareness of, the phonological structure of the words' in language (1994: 276). In a large-scale longitudinal study of 5-year-old children moving from kindergarten through the first two years of school, they identified three discrete aspects of skill in phonological processing, with two aspects having sub-groups. The first was phonological awareness, comprising two distinct but correlated areas: phonological analysis and phonological synthesis.

Phonological analysis describes the ability to identify or isolate phonemes from words presented as wholes. It can be measured in young children by tasks such as identifying rhymes or identifying by listening, words that start or end with the same phoneme. It can be measured in older children by harder tasks which involve them saying the first phoneme of a word when given a picture; or saying which new word is made when one sound is omitted, for example, if the 'l' is removed from the word 'slit'; or via 'spoonerisms', where the first phonemes of two words are transposed (for example, 'riding boot' becomes 'biding root'). The younger children's tasks involve providing them with examples to think about, whereas older children are asked to process words 'in their heads'.

Phonological synthesis is the ability to blend phonemes presented separately back into whole words. It can be measured by tasks that say words as individual phonemes and ask children to re-synthesize them into words, for example 'd' 'o' 'g' into 'dog'.

Torgesen et al. (1994) also identified two other aspects of phonological skill: phonological memory and phonological access, with access divided into two sub-groups. Phonological memory involves the brief retention in working memory of non-meaningful auditory sequences, such as letters, digits or spoken non-words. It is assumed that memory for such items is primarily phonologically based, as phonemes have to be decoded quickly to remember the items with no support from meaning. It can be measured by asking children to remember digits or letters, or to repeat non-words.

Phonological access measures how rapidly phonological information stored in the lexicon (word bank) can be retrieved, and is measured by rapid naming tasks. Phonological access was sub-divided into two discrete sets of skills. Serial naming is the ability to name common items rapidly, measured by presenting children with simple and well-known pictures, letters or numbers to name as fast as they could. Torgesen used letters and digits, but well-known nouns can be used instead, such as 'key', 'comb', 'pen', 'ring', 'book', 'cup', 'cat' and 'spoon'. These are pictured on a chequer-board in random order, and children asked to name them rapidly one after the other, so that phonological forms must be accessed very quickly. Isolated naming involves a similar task, but with items presented one at a time on a computer screen.

Torgesen et al. (1994) discuss the three main phonological skills – awareness, memory and access – as together comprising 'phonological processing'. Phonological processing abilities and difficulties seemed to be fairly stable child characteristics, with phonological awareness in particular strongly related to subsequent reading skills.

The development of phonological awareness and its relationship to reading

Phonological awareness develops during childhood, with a move towards breaking words up into smaller and smaller segments (reviewed by Stone et al., 1998). Children first identify whole words; then they can break some compound words like 'cowboy', 'greenhouse' or 'toothbrush' into their separate component words; then they can break some words into syllables; then into 'onset' and 'rime'. 'Onset' is the consonants (if any) at the beginning of the syllable before the first vowel, and 'rime' is the rest, comprising the vowel and any consonants after it to the end of the syllable. Examples are:

Syllable	Onset	Rime
all	(none)	all
tall	t	all
crawl	cr	awl
split	spl	it
paw	p	aw

Breaking words up in this way may be one of the ways in which children learn to perceive 'rhymes', words where the onset differs but the rime does not. The third stage in phonological awareness involves breaking a word into phonemes, so that the child can tell which phoneme starts a word, and later which ends it, and can split up clusters into their component consonants. This demonstrates conscious awareness of a word's phonological form.

The interest in phonological awareness among teachers of literacy is due to the strong relationship that exists between success on phonological awareness tasks and success with reading, both when measured concurrently or when phonological awareness is measured first, when it predicts later reading skill. Children who do badly on phonological awareness tasks often have trouble with literacy attainments. Castles and Coltheart (2004) review the research literature, and comment upon the strength of this relationship. They caution, however, that correlation does not imply a causal relationship. Some other factor could be causing both phonological awareness and literacy to be relatively advanced or delayed. Furthermore, phonological awareness may not be a pre-existing, 'non-reading precursor to reading', but develop as children are introduced to letter–sound correspondences as part of their early reading experiences. Phonemic awareness skills 'are rarely in evidence in the absence of alphabetic skills' (Castles and Coltheart, 2004), suggesting a reciprocal rather than a causal relationship. This idea is compatible with the work of Morais et al. (1979), who found that adults from a non-literate culture who had never been introduced to reading were not very good at the phonological awareness task of adding or deleting a phoneme at the start of a non-word, whilst adults from the same culture who had learned to read as a child or adult had little difficulty. The ability to consciously manipulate phonology may be less causally connected to reading than is sometimes assumed, and both phonological awareness and literacy activities need to be fostered, but a lack of skill in phonological awareness is not a good sign for learning to read and spell.

Assessing phonological processing skills

Since phonological processing skills may give clues as to the facility with which children will develop reading, teachers are often interested in investigating this area. There are two main approaches: assessing a child's phonological processing skills separately from literacy skills, and analysing their reading and written work for evidence of phonologically-based confusions.

Assessing phonological processing skills directly

Some assessments are informal, such as the pack developed in the READ Project in Dundee (Kemp and Peters, 2003), which provides informal information on how a child copes with tasks such as rhyme detection. Teachers can ask children to say whether two words rhyme; or to spot the 'odd one out' from two words that rhyme and one that does not; or to say which is the first and/or last consonant in a word, to get an idea of how aware a child is of the phonological structure of words.

However, phonological skills develop as children become older, and assessment tasks need to measure how a child is coping in comparison with children of their own age. For these purposes a standardized assessment is best: 'home-made' tasks might present activities that are too hard or too easy and so draw inappropriate conclusions. If a teacher thinks, on the basis of informal assessments, that a child might have a problem they can use a standardized measure. There are standardized assessments available for teachers' use covering all aspects of phonological skill development between the ages of three years and 24 years (including Dodd et al., 2000; Frederickson et al., 1997; Muter et al., 1997; Torgesen and Bryant 2004; Wagner et al., 1999). Using such measures allows real problems to be spotted, and a child's progress to be tracked over time.

Analysing reading and writing

Children who get stuck at the alphabetic stage of literacy are calling upon their internalized, auditory-based phonological representations, and over-regularizing the orthographic system of English to try to make a fit. Stone et al. (1998) suggest looking at the errors children make when reading and writing, to see if they could have a phonological basis. A child writing 'has' as 'haz' is reflecting the accurate phonological form of the word, and a child writing 'fote' for 'vote' is only reflecting a slight error in the timing of voicing between voiced-voiceless twin phonemes. Errors that are often put down to visual confusions could be due to phonological slips – such as 'p/b', 'm/n', 'b/d' – and vowels will often be written using a letter that *does* represent the vowel sound, but not in the word being tackled. Listening to a child attempting to read a word aloud will also give clues as to how a child is processing text. 'Closed class' grammar words and markers deserve particularly close attention. A child who spells words as they are 'in their head' does not have a phonological problem, but may need to be taught a lot of spelling rules.

Focused teaching

A large number of studies have combined training in phonological awareness with teaching of reading-related skills such as letter–sound correspondence, and shown increases in reading attainment (see Castles and Coltheart, 2004). The fact that phonological awareness and alphabetic knowledge have a reciprocal relationship argues against teaching either aspect on its own, or even preceding letter teaching with phonological awareness training. Teaching both together appears to be most profitable.

There is similarly no reason to assume that a child with demonstrably poor phonological awareness cannot learn to read, although they may need extra support to do so. Many teaching packs exist. Teachers use phonological awareness activities to capitalize on the existing phonological representations a child brings to the reading process to anchor the complicated orthographic information needed to become competent readers and writers. Analysing errors and confusions provides teaching ideas as well as assessing difficulties, and can be used as teaching points to explain irregularities and variations.

Ensuring that new words encountered in the curriculum are discussed in relation to their phonological form as well as their meaning is also important (McCartney et al., 2005). Discussing how many syllables are in a word; what it rhymes with; what sounds (not just letters) are at the beginning and end; and if there are any 'little words' within it can help to 'fix' the word in the child's lexicon. When discussing word meanings, linking a word to its root can sometimes explain spelling peculiarities. Most children do not need to change their internal phonological representations but can be helped to apply their tacit knowledge to acquiring literacy skills. Teachers have opportunity to capitalize on this knowledge to support children in the sustained effort required to master the maddening variations in the English orthographic system.

SOMETHING TO THINK ABOUT

- Read a piece of writing by a child carefully. If they are making consistent errors (between, for example, 'p' and 'b' or 's' and 'z'), consider the possibility that these may be based on the phonemes rather than a visual confusion between letter shapes.
- Think about the children in your class. Are there any that seem to struggle with phonics? Could any of these have phonological problems?

SOMETHING TO READ

- Castles, A. and Coltheart, M. (2004) 'Is there a causal link from phonological awareness to success in learning to read?', *Cognition*, 9(1): 77–111, gives a detailed account of the relationship between phonological processing and reading.
- Martin, D. (2000) *Teaching Children with Speech and Language Difficulties*. London: David Fulton, gives introductory information on speech development and difficulties for teachers.

SOMETHING TO DO

- Think about the movements you are making with each part of your mouth as you say the words 'standby', 'surfboarding' and 'thermometer' aloud a number of times, very slowly. Now say them again, but quickly this time. What differences do you notice?
- Listen carefully to your children to see if they use voiceless 'th' or 'f' in words like 'thumb', 'Catherine', 'teeth', 'nothing'. You might even hear 'h' in some.

Chapter 7

Phonics in Context: Spelling Links

Laura Huxford

The relationship of phonics to spelling has been as contentious as that of phonics to reading. There are those who vehemently eschew any association of phonics and spelling on the basis that encouraging children to 'write words as they sound' invariably results in incorrect spelling. There are, on the other hand, strong advocates of phonically-based spelling programmes. However, in almost all research commentary on reading development and teaching literacy in the last 20 years, the phrase 'phonics is necessary but not sufficient' continues to be reiterated (see, for example, Stanovich, 1980; Tunmer, 1991; National Reading Panel, 2000a; DfES, 2005a). As John Stannard says, phonics is a heuristic device to enable children to grasp the fundamentals of the alphabetic system (Stannard and Huxford, forthcoming).

Just as the teaching of writing is less prominent in research and media coverage than the teaching of reading, so phonics for spelling has taken second place to phonics for reading. However, there is considerable research going back to Isabelle Liberman and colleagues in the 1970s to show that the skill of phonemic segmentation, which is the skill required for 'phonic spelling', is also critical to the development of phonemic blending, a skill required for reading. Further research suggests that it may well be a precursor to it (Frith, 1985; Cataldo and Ellis, 1988; Huxford et al., 1991). For this and other reasons, the guidance on teaching phonics in the National Literacy Strategy proposed that phonemic segmentation be introduced before phonemic blending.

In this chapter I will argue that in learning to be literate in English, early spelling *is* largely phonics and that, conversely, early phonics *is* spelling. I will briefly sketch out the place of phonics in the process and acquisition of spelling and explain why it is appropriate to introduce phonics through spelling. I will give examples of how an understanding of children's spelling development and the various 'logics' behind the spellings of words can help teachers to analyse and understand pupils' misspellings and suggest an approach to teaching spelling which builds on phonics.

The place of phonics in the process and acquisition of spelling

The term 'phonics' is shorthand for an element of the curriculum which covers teaching and learning the alphabetic system or code – the correspondences between phonemes and graphemes – and the skills of segmentation and blending. It is also used to denote the use of phonemic processes to read and spell.

Various psychological models have been suggested to account for how we read and write, but in essence we probably draw upon some sort of visual store of words which we have accumulated over time as we have repeatedly encountered and used them. The accuracy with which we retrieve words from this personal store is more crucial for spelling than reading. Most of us would agree that there are words that we can read with no difficulty but that when required to write them we cannot recall every letter with total accuracy. Common examples include 'gauge', 'separate' and 'accommodate'. Most people try out a number of versions of the word to be spelled and select the one that 'looks right'. However, we also have words in our spoken vocabulary that we have not encountered in texts very often and therefore have not created secure mental images of them. When writing such a word we tend to spell it by analogy on the basis of the syllabic structure of another similar sounding word and then represent remaining phonemes with the most likely graphemes. The spelling options are further reduced by considering other words that are related in meaning. For example, on the basis of the phonemic structure, the 'y' in the spoken word 'pyroclastic' could reasonably be spelled with an 'i' and the unstressed 'o' with any vowel, for example 'piraclastic' or 'pirerclastic'. But the meaning of the word suggests that the first four letters relate to other words such as 'pyrotechnic' and 'pyromaniac', which would lead the writer to spell the word correctly with 'y' and 'o'. Similarly, plant enthusiasts, familiar with the form of Latin plant names, would be likely to write correctly the name of any plant that they had heard about but never encountered in print. Thus, even experienced spellers use a phonemic approach to spelling, usually overlaid with another strategy, when writing unfamiliar words.

For young children very few words are familiar. But in the English language, which is an alphabetic system, they do have the rudimentary building blocks for spelling words. Young children who are taught or who deduce elements of the alphabetic code make very good use of it to spell. Read (1986), Bissex (1980) and Gentry (1982) catalogued examples of children's propensity to break (segment) words into phonemes and find appropriate letters to represent the sounds they identified. Most teachers of young children can furnish the visitor with examples (such as those shown in Figure 7.1 on p. 89).

Young children's efforts at spelling are based on a keen analysis of the sounds they hear within words so, for instance, the word 'new' may be spelled 'niyoo'. Their efforts are also based on an emerging and usually idiosyncratic knowledge of sound–symbol correspondences. Letters are pressed into service in unconventional ways, so upper-case N might be used as its name which is pronounced 'en' after 'h' to spell 'hen' (hN) (Ferreiro and Teberovsky, 1982). However, they do not confine themselves to representations based on sounds in words. As Gunther Kress illustrates in his book *Early Spelling* (2000), very young children also employ pictures and other symbols to convey their message. (This approach to writing – linking the written form directly to the meaning of words – will be partially regained when the writer understands more fully the complexities of English orthography.) Nevertheless, the use of phonics to spell has three advantages for the developing writer: words can be spelled without recourse to anyone else; the system is flexible as the same letters are used over again to make any word; and each word does not have to be memorized. Although the spelling may not be correct, it is usually decodable by a persistent reader, particularly when the writer has attained the stage of representing vowel sounds.

These were the arguments used in the early 1980s by researchers and teacher practitioners in the United States and also in England during the National Writing Project to support 'developmental writing' or 'invented spelling' – although the recognition that this was phonic spelling was not widely acknowledged. Running concurrently across the United Kingdom, and stemming originally from the research of Margaret Peters that spelling should be 'taught not caught' (Peters, 1985), was the message that spelling was primarily a visuo-kinaesthetic skill (Cripps, 1991) with the dictum 'Look, cover, write, check'. There was legitimate concern in the profession that children who are allowed to only 'spell as they hear' will practise bad habits and internalize incorrect spellings. This is an example of the age-old conflict between allowing children to pursue their learning in step with what is perceived as their 'natural' development and trammelling their learning to avoid potential confusion. The issue here, as I have already indicated, is that even experienced writers need a phonemic spelling strategy to spell unfamiliar words. So, not allowing children to explore phonics in relation to spelling would reduce their strategies for spelling these words. But in encouraging phonics in the early stage, children must be helped to realize that other factors override the simple orthography generated from phonological correspondences. In England, the National Literacy Strategy made an explicit attempt to resolve this conflict by recognizing the value of phonics to spelling, but also stressing the significance of morphology and etymology (DfEE, 1998a; DfES, in press).

The place of spelling in the acquisition of phonics

In the relationship between phonics and spelling, the National Literacy Strategy (NLS) actually went further. Not only did it recognize the importance of phonics to spelling, it also saw spelling as pivotal to phonics. At the time, phonics was associated more with the special educational needs curriculum than mainstream. Generally, phonics was taught to enable children to blend for reading. However, the research consistently showed a strong correlation between success in segmentation and successful reading (Liberman, 1971; Liberman et al., 1974; Lundberg et al., 1980). Reading Recovery was one of the earliest programmes to include segmentation, and more recent phonics programmes such as THRASS™ and Phonographix© place segmentation at the fore.

In mainstream early years education, developmental writing, also known as 'invented spelling', was highly regarded. It was viewed as a more motivating approach for children than dictating what they wanted to say and then copying the teacher's writing. But on the whole, teachers did not make a connection between the processes in developmental writing and phonics. The NLS professional development materials brought the two together. In the teacher training material (DfEE, 1998b), in *Progression in Phonics* (DfEE, 1999a) and in *Playing with Sounds* (DfEE, 2003a) there was early emphasis on segmentation and letter knowledge, followed by blending for reading.

There was a growing body of research and pedagogic argument to support this position. Building on the research showing the importance of segmentation cited above, were developmental studies indicating that children acquire the skill of segmentation slightly in advance of the skill of blending. Anecdotal evidence for this can be found as long ago as the writing of Montessori (1912, 1964), and Chomsky (1979) proposed that children should learn to spell before learning to read to capitalize on their early propensity to hear sounds in words. Empirical evidence that children could spell phonemically-regular words that they could not read was contained in a study by Bryant and Bradley in 1980. Frith (1985) proposed a model of learning (Table 7.1) to read and spell in which she proposed that spelling was the pacemaker for reading. Subsequently, longitudinal studies by Cataldo and Ellis (1988) and Huxford et al. (1991) showed a developmental progression in which children's ability to spell phonemically-regular words preceded their being able to read them.

Based on much of the literature of the period, for example Ehri (1984), Frith's model traces developmental progressions for reading and writing: children's earliest writing consisting of pictures as symbols for words, events or messages; a logographic stage where children read and write words they have memorized as shapes, such as their names and signs; an alphabetic (phonic) stage; and finally an orthographic stage when knowledge of morphology facilitates reading and writing. Many teachers and parents recognize these stages in children.

The fascinating element of this model is that the stages do not occur in parallel for reading and writing. The logographic stage in writing appears short-lived; children abandon it in favour of using a phonic approach. The phonic stage in reading starts after the phonic stage in writing. In practice this means that children latch onto the alphabetic principle and begin to write words as they sound. In phonemically-regular short-vowelled words such as 'bat', 'hot'

Step	Writing	Reading
1a	symbolic	logographic
1b	logographic	logographic
2a	alphabetic	logographic
2b	alphabetic	alphabetic
3a	alphabetic	orthographic
3b	orthographic	orthographic

Table 7.1   **The six-step model of skills in reading and writing acquisition (Frith, 1985)**

and 'fig', this strategy will produce correct spellings so long as the children's knowledge of letters is adequate. However, if the words are not in their visual lexicons, they probably will not be able to read them as their blending ability may not be sufficiently developed. The National Literacy Strategy capitalized on the need for letters in developmental writing and used the purpose for writing as the vehicle for learning phonics.

Understanding children's spelling

There is evidence to suggest that, given favourable circumstances, young children are motivated to write – to imitate those around them by making squiggles on paper or to attempt to convey a message (Temple et al., 1988; Ferreiro and Teberovsky, 1982; Kress, 2000). In addition to wavy lines that are akin to adult joined handwriting, they will use pictures and symbols that they encounter in their lives, most notably approximations of numbers and letters. They ascribe meaning to the marks they make and may use a consistent group of symbols to represent a meaning more than once in their writing. The child's concept of a word – the awareness of a discrete entity known as 'a word' – is still in its early development. However, the concept of breaking the stream of speech into discrete words is probably enhanced by seeing names and labels written down. Furthermore, there is no relationship between the marks they make and the sound or phonemic properties of the spoken form of the message. In fact, the concept of a word and the realization of a connection between spoken language and its written form seem to be closely allied (Morris, 1993). The recognition that words share common sounds and that these are represented by the same symbol in writing is pivotal and is essentially the first step in 'spelling'.

At first children will use letters to represent some sounds as well as other marks or random letters. When they start to use letters exclusively to represent the phonemic properties of the message, they are likely to write a string of letters representing the prominent phonemes at the beginning of some words and syllables. For example, a child might write 'Iwtsmgm' ('I went to see my granma').

Consonant phonemes are easier to hear than vowels, and so for a short period young children may fill out their words but only with consonants. For example, 'Sm cm hm wv m ysd' ('Sam came home with me yesterday'). The addition of vowels and the incorporation of words they know well from their reading make the writing much easier to read and lift children's perceptions of themselves as independent writers: 'I wet to the pub wiv mi dad and mi mum and I had sum cris' ('I went to the pub with my dad and my mum and I had some crisps'). The consonants 'n' and 'm' are quite difficult to hear next to another consonant, so these often appear later.

Of course, the children's aural perception of the phonemes in a spoken word dictates which phonemes they represent. This can work in both directions: over-representing, such as 'nyoo' for 'new', and under-representing, such as 'sepret' for 'separate'. The examples in Figure 7.1 are from personal narratives by 4- and 5-year-old children.

In example (a), ros dinr (roast dinner), the child has not heard the letter 't' in roast as the two words elide. Children make letters work hard. In example (b), Choclt (chocolate), the letter 'l' represents the /l/ phoneme and the following unaccented vowel – perfectly logical when the child calls this letter sound 'lu'. Similarly in example (c), 'I went to the prk. I went wiv mi mum and mi dad' ('I went to the park. I went with my mum and my dad'), the child spells the 'ar' phoneme in 'park' with the letter 'r', using the name rather than the sound of the letter.

Some confusions are quite common, according to the research literature. For instance, children regularly spell words beginning with 'tr' such as 'train' with 'chr', thus writing 'chrain', or 'chrip'. In examples (d) – (f) children's pronunciation shows clearly through their writing.

In example (d), 'At the weekend I went to Cheltenham wiv miy Dad and miy mum and miy siststu and miy buvu' ('At the weekend I went to Cheltenham with my Dad and my mum and my sister and my brother'), the child shows his pronunciation of 'th' as 'v' in 'with' and 'brother' and exaggerates the /ie/ in 'my' so hearing a /y/ sound at the end. But he is consistent in his spelling (or misspelling) of the word.

In example (e), 'I went to the park and I fell off the mugky bars and bumt my herd and I had a big bump on my herd' ('I went to the park and I fell off the monkey bars and bumped my head and I had a big bump on my head'), for the word 'monkey' the child has used the letter 'g' to capture the illusive 'ng' phoneme, which is a correct representation of how the word is usually pronounced. We do not tend to say 'munky'; we actually pronounce it mungky. Similarly she has not represented the 'p' in bumped because she does not pronounce or hear it with a 'p'. But when she comes to 'bump' she can hear the 'p'.

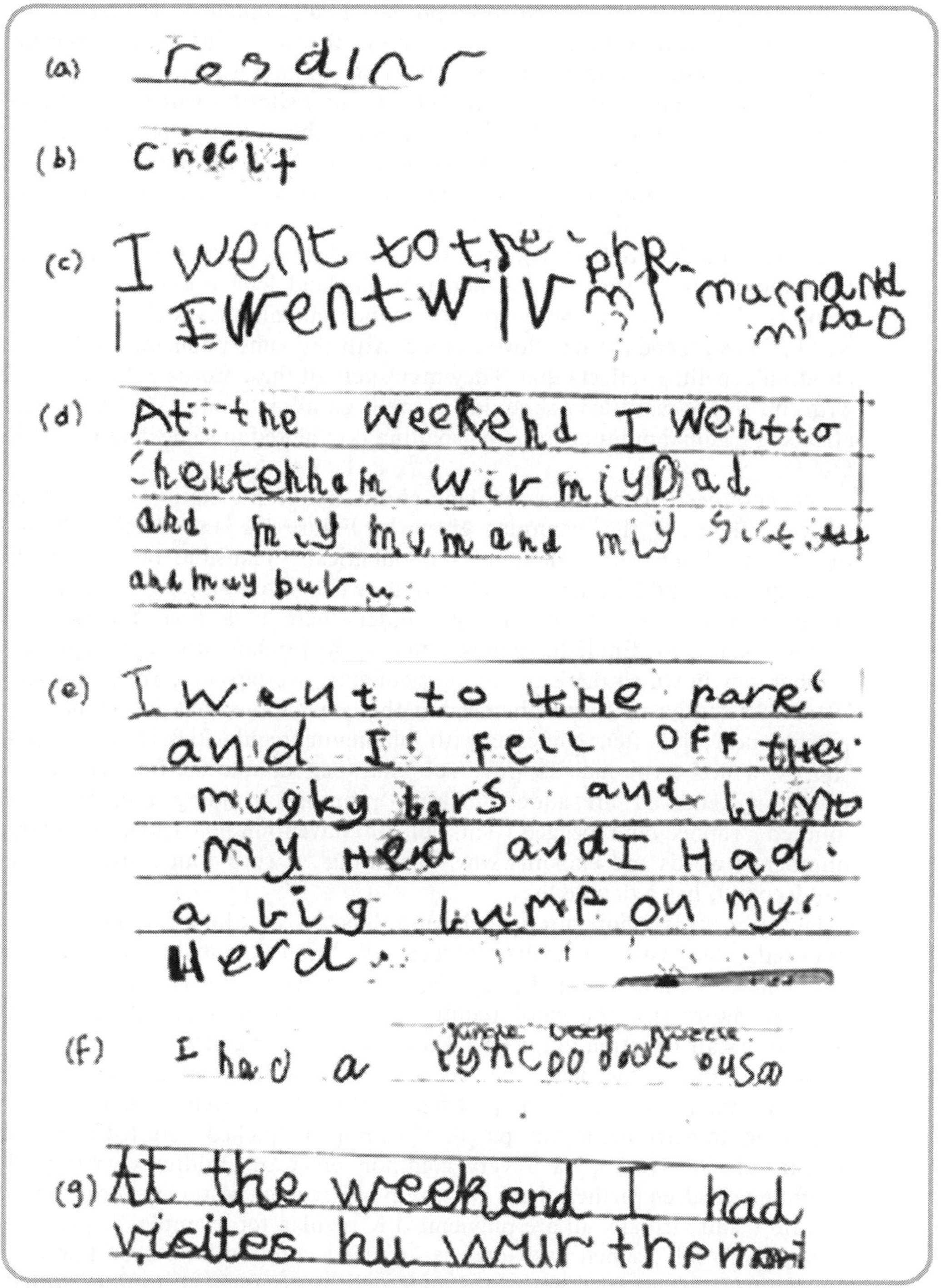

(a) readinr

(b) cnoclt

(c) I went to the prr
i I wentwiv mr mumand
ni Dad

(d) At the weekend I wehtto
Cheltenham wirmiyDad
and miy mum and miy sit
and may butu

(e) I went to the pare
and I fell off the
mugky bars and lump
my hed and I Had
a big lump on my
Herd

(f) I had a runcoodort ouso

(g) At the weekend I had
visites hu wmur theman

Figure 7.1   Examples of children's spellings

In example (f), 'I had a juncoo booc pusoo' ('I had a jungle book puzzle'), you can hear the child losing the 'le' at the end of the words 'jungle' and 'puzzle', and he is consistent in spelling the 'le' with 'oo' in both words.

The final example (g), 'At the weekend I had visites hu wur the next door nebus' ('At the weekend I had visitors who were the next door neighbours'), is from a girl rising six years old who has taken to joined writing with ease and seems totally comfortable in writing any word she wishes by inventing phonemically plausible spellings.

These examples are from children in a school in the south-west of England. Examples from children in the north of England look different in certain respects. For instance, some people pronounce the middle vowel of the words 'wool', 'book', 'hood', 'mug', 'love', 'come' with the same phoneme, and young children's spelling reflects this. They may spell all these words with 'oo' or all with 'u', so the word 'come' could be spelt 'cum' or 'coom'. The interesting effects of regional pronunciation on spelling is explored in some detail in Wells (2001).

Teachers need to be aware of how children's pronunciation affects their early spelling. In the examples given in Figure 7.1 and detailed above, in almost all the words there is a phonemically plausible reason for the spelling. The children try really hard to write intelligibly and should be congratulated. However, as they get older there is a need for them to accommodate to English orthography – a fundamentally morphemic orthography in which there are strong phonemic overlaps or correspondences. Words are composed of morphemes but the conventions that govern how the morphemes join often coincide with phonemic regularities. For example, short-vowelled verbs such as 'pin', 'rub' and 'beg' double the final consonant when 'ing' and 'ed' are added, making 'pinning', 'rubbing' and 'begging', 'pinned', 'rubbed' and 'begged'. This rule or convention holds good for a large number of words and explains why 'beginning', a word which often catches children out, has a double 'n'.

However, this phonemic convention has to sit alongside morphemic knowledge of past-tense verbs. In 'begged', 'pinned' and 'rubbed' the /d/ phoneme is sounded immediately after the preceding consonant. The child must be aware that the word requires the morpheme 'ed', not just 'd', to describe a state or action in the past. But, in verbs ending in 't' and 'd' ('rented', 'shouted', landed, 'needed') the 'ed' sounds like 'id', and unless children recognize the need to mark the past tense with 'ed', they tend to write 'rentid' and so on. In verbs ending in 'p', 'k', 'f' ('jumped', 'picked', 'stuffed'), the 'ed' sounds like 't'; 'jumpt' is a very common error in children's writing. To confound children further, there is a group of irregular past tense verbs that do end in 't' and virtually all are phonemically regular, for example, 'kept', 'felt', 'sent', 'lost', 'left'. When past tense is insecure, children have been known to apply this convention to non-verbs and spell words such as 'soft' as 'soffed'. Peter Bryant and Terezinha Nunes have accumulated a significant corpus of research on the effects of grammar and morphology on children's spelling and teachers' knowledge of morphology (Bryant et al., 1997; Bryant et al., 2000; Bryant, 2002; Nunes et al., 2003; Hurry et al., 2005).

Applying the research: teaching and learning spelling

The relationship between research on children as spellers and the policy and practice for teaching spelling is complex and often poorly articulated. A study of the National Literacy Strategy in England indicates that this is not inevitable, however. The first stage in learning to spell is learning phonics and, as explained earlier, the first step in learning phonics is to use it to spell. That phonics has a purpose in enabling children to be independent writers was the key approach taken by the first professional development materials in the National Literacy Strategy in 1998. *Progression in Phonics* (DfEE, 1999a) then aimed at speeding up children's acquisition of letter knowledge and the ability to segment for spelling as well as blending for reading. It parcelled learning phonics into seven steps. The first three were steps in segmentation, letter knowledge came in at step 2 and from step 4 onwards blending was included. Step 1 covers general phonological development including playing with rhyme and alliteration (recognition that the phrase 'Suzy slices saucy sausages' contains an abundance of the 'sss' sound). Step 2 uses segmenting the initial consonant in words to learn a handful of letters. Step 3 moves on to segmenting the final sound in a consonant–vowel–consonant (CVC) word through which more letters are learned. At Step 4 children learn the vowel letters in the process of learning how to segment the medial vowel in CVC words. Through segmenting and spelling CVC words, children learn how to blend the sounds of letters into words for reading. Step 5 introduces consecutive consonants at the beginning and end of words, again the blending of consonants being learned through prior experience of their segmentation. Long vowels are introduced in Step 6, with one representation for each vowel so that children could use long vowels to spell, the major work on vowel choices being left to Step 7. A professional development CD-ROM was produced for teachers in 2000 (DfEE, 2000).

This guidance was supplemented five years later by *Playing with Sounds* (DfES, 2003a), a set of teaching cards and a CD-ROM. In the intervening period, the inspectorate reported that the quality of phonics teaching in England had improved. Teachers were finding that most children were able to segment the medial vowel much more readily than children in previous years, and were concerned that blending was left too late. In the light of this feedback steps 2, 3 and 4 were condensed, but the process for learning letters was still through spelling, followed immediately by blending for reading.

The essence of all the NLS materials is that phonics should be systematically taught in a playful manner. Games were developed for the materials in which children manipulate concrete objects, not simply pictures, where they move around the room and interact with each other as well as adults. *Playing with Sounds* also includes a large number of examples where adults have taken the opportunity to extend the children's learning within activities that the children have initiated.

Although the use of phonics empowers children when writing independently, some children find the effort of forming letters deters them from writing. These children need support in developing their fine motor skills so that they can take part in an activity which they would be more likely to relish if the physical side was not such an obstacle. *Developing Early Writing* (DfES, 2001) suggests ways of offering this support as well as providing ideas for helping children to internalize the letter movements through gross motor activities. While these (and other) children are improving their handwriting skills, they can be purposefully writing using small keyboards, magnetic letters or, better still, an interactive whiteboard where they can select letters and move them around on the screen. Unlike magnetic letters, letters on an electronic whiteboard cannot run out!

Phonics, however, is only part of the story in learning to spell. Recognizing how words are structured is arguably the first step in securing a personal vocabulary of words. The NLS five-session spelling programme for 7- and 8-year-old children (DfES, 2001) assumes that realistically, teachers will devote five teaching sessions over a fortnight to teaching spelling and that at least two of these will be extended to include independent work by the children and be the subject of a follow-up whole class plenary session.

The five sessions allow for teaching the structure of words, attention to spelling age-appropriate vocabulary by analysing the structure and identifying the 'tricky' parts of words that are likely to be difficult to remember. An equally important part of the programme is practice and application, so that as well as understanding how words are constructed, children retain them in memory for use in writing when they need to pay as much attention as possible to composition, not transcription.

The programme uses investigation and problem solving as the basis for learning how words are constructed. These investigations take the form of games such as 'Word sort', 'Guess my word', 'Add race' and 'Find your team'. The approach taken to learning how to commit words to memory is to ask the question 'Why is this word spelled like this?' The work on word structure helps children to answer this question. But sometimes children need to spell words that have an irregular feature. Children are encouraged to find parts of the word that fit a convention and then to decide upon some way to remember the 'tricky' part. For instance, the notorious word 'yacht' has three phonemes, two of which are spelled perfectly regularly. The /o/ phoneme is represented by three very unusual letters. People invent different ways to recall this group of letters. Some prefer to visualize the shape, others to say the letter names, others to create a mnemonic. The process of analysing it into three phonemes with an 'odd middle' goes a long way to helping children remember it.

Phonemic analysis helps towards understanding the structure of words. Morphemic analysis, as described earlier, is also essential. The reason the word 'accommodate' has two sets of double letters is because it is a series of morphemes, each of which needs to be written in full – 'ac-com-mod-ate'. The origins of words (etymology) provide reasons for their spelling. Another well-used example is the relationship between the words 'sign' and 'signal'; the pronounced 'g' in 'signal' is an etymological mnemonic for the unpronounced 'g' in 'sign'. Like all problem-solving activities, children are fascinated by word study of this sort.

Conclusion

Writing, spelling or 'making words' has an important role to play in learning phonics because it provides the motivation as well as the analytic component that drives phonics for reading. Conversely, phonics plays an important role in spelling. At first it is the liberating element to young children's writing and as they develop, children need to realize that there is more to spelling than phonics. However, as one of the features of a word's structure, phonics remains an important component in spelling.

SOMETHING TO THINK ABOUT

- Look at Frith's model of the development of spelling and reading (Table 7.1). Does this relate to your experiences of working with young children?

SOMETHING TO READ

- DfES (2003b) *Year 2 and 3 Planning Exemplification and Spelling Programme*, Reference no. 0493-2003. London: DfES. Available online at http://www.standards.dfes.gov.uk/primary/publications/literacy/849451/
- Chapter 8 in this book, 'Phonics and English Orthography' by Henrietta Dombey.
- Chapter 6 in this book, 'Developmental Issues: Speaking and Phonological Awareness' by Elspeth McCartney.

SOMETHING TO DO

- Try spelling some words that you have heard but are not sure how to spell. What strategies do you use? Check the spellings in a dictionary. If there are places where you have gone wrong, try to work out why this is.

- Identify a child in your class who is a poor speller. Use the key ideas in this chapter to list what this child does know and understand about spelling and identify some of the things that the child has yet to learn. Pick the single thing that you think will give the biggest overall learning pay-off for this child and make this a teaching priority.

Chapter 8

Phonics and English Orthography

Henrietta Dombey

The teaching and learning of phonics have to be set in context. Before we can make a decision about the suitability of a synthetic phonic approach to the teaching of reading, we need to consider what it is that children have to learn. Others have discussed what is involved in learning to read in terms of comprehension and putting reading to use (see Chapters 1 and 4). These considerations are vitally important for all children learning to read, all over the world. However, in this chapter I am looking at what is involved in learning to read English: at the difficulties encountered and the support given, the challenges and the opportunities offered by the peculiarities of English spelling – the *orthography* of written English.

Does the orthography of a language make a difference?

Is it harder to learn to read English than other languages? The brief answer is 'probably yes', if we're talking about other languages with an alphabetic script. The idea of an alphabet is, of course, that it is *phonographic*, that is the written signs represent speech sounds, rather than *logographic*, where the written signs stand for the meanings of the words represented. In a 'pure' alphabetic system, each letter represents a *phoneme*, the smallest unit of speech sound that makes a difference to meaning. The word 'cat' is an example of a purely phonographic English word: the spoken word has three phonemes, each of which serves to distinguish it from other words such as 'mat', 'cot' and 'can', and each of which is represented in the written word by a single letter of the alphabet. If all English words were spelled like this, we could say we had a 'pure' alphabetic system of writing. But as we all know, this is not typical of English spelling.

Many of the languages of continental Europe have a fairly reliable match between letters and phonemes. In Italian, for example, the 25 phonemes of spoken Italian are represented by 24 single letters (no 'k' or 'y') and 8 letter combinations, such as 'ch', where English might use 'k'. Italian and other languages with a similarly straightforward relationship between phonemes and letters are said to have a *transparent* or *shallow* orthography. In contrast, English has an *opaque* or *deep* orthography. In the English writing system some 461 *graphemes* – letters or letter combinations – represent some 40 to 45 phonemes (the number varies according to your accent and your procedure of classification). Because of interference from other factors, such as the age of starting schooling, the teaching approach adopted and the part played by the written word in different societies, it's very difficult to isolate the contribution played by orthography to the speed and ease with which young children learn to read. Researchers have found that children do seem slower to learn to read in languages with deep orthographies. In line with children in many countries of continental Europe, most Italian children master the basics of word recognition in only six months of schooling (Cossu et al., 1995). But it has been estimated that the deep orthography of English adds two to three years to the process for children learning to read in English (Seymour et al., 2003). It also takes longer for individuals to process deep orthographies and appears to involve different parts of the brain (Paulesu et al., 2000). We need to look at the orthography of English to know how this deep orthography is constructed – what the complexities are that children have to learn.

Attempts to bring order to chaos

The 'common-sense' view is that the English spelling system is chaotic, and that the deviation of many spellings from the phonographic principle is largely the result of significant changes to pronunciation, coupled with marked conservatism in the written language. But how true is this? How chaotic is English spelling? Is it the result of a combination of oral flexibility and written rigidity?

Certainly a number of attempts have been made to rationalize English spelling, to make it more phonographic. In the last century the most notable have been the Shavian extended alphabet devised by Kingsley Read in 1959 (MacCarthy, 1969) and the Initial Teaching Alphabet (Downing, 1965). The Shavian extended alphabet was the result of a large bequest left by George Bernard Shaw for this purpose. It consists of 48 invented letters, each one consistently representing a phoneme of *received pronunciation* (the high-status accent sometimes known as 'BBC English'), but none resembling any letters of the Roman alphabet. It would seem that this totally transparent orthography was nevertheless too strange to those already familiar with conventional English spelling in Roman letters, so made little impact. Working on a different principle, the Initial Teaching Alphabet (ITA), invented by Sir James Pitman, took the letters of the Roman alphabet as its base, supplementing these with further invented letters so that every phoneme could be represented unambiguously. ITA flourished in the 1960s, but gradually withered, perhaps as a result of the dissatisfaction experienced by parents, children and some teachers at the lack of continuity between children's experience of print at home and at school. Extending the alphabet and regularizing English spelling appear to be non-trivial matters, not easily accomplished.

Certainly, the orthography of English is essentially alphabetic. *At base the English writing system works by representing phonemes with graphemes.* This is the first key feature of English orthography, and, at its most straightforward, it gives us words such as 'cat' and 'chip'. But many English words don't quite work in this way.

Some historical influences

History has, of course, shaped our spelling. The spelling of words such as 'knight' and 'lamb' reflect the rather different pronunciation of their Anglo-Saxon ancestry. Over the centuries the pronunciation of words has shifted, but their spelling has remained relatively constant. But it's not just the history of changing pronunciation growing away from stable spelling that has shaped the orthography of English. A stronger influence seems to be the many words imported from other languages that have brought with them rather different spelling patterns (Sampson, 1985).

Complexity has marked English spelling for nearly a thousand years. Before the Norman invasion, the language of what is now England was Old English, with a number of regional variants. But there was a standard written system, based on the language of Wessex (Sampson, 1985). This was the language of official documents, and thus very unusual in Europe, as elsewhere Latin continued to serve the purpose of official transactions. This written English operated to a set of rules that made it largely phonographic, in other words, it operated with a nearly transparent orthography.

But with the large-scale imports of Norman French from the 11th century onwards, came a different set of patterns. The two contrasting spelling patterns can be seen very clearly in pairs of homophones such as 'shoot' and 'chute', 'ark' and 'arc', 'root' and 'route', 'mussel' and 'muscle' (Carney, 1994). As Carney observes, the two sets of spellings represent not only their origins in different orthographies, governed by different sets of spelling rules, but also 'different semantic fields and different ranges of experience' (Carney, 1994: 96). As he points out, if you want to make a colloquial form of the word 'lunatic', you spell it 'loony' or 'looney', not 'luny'. In the unregulated plethora of spellings for English that followed 1066, many writers used the new French patterns on words from Old English. Some of these 'Frenchified' spellings endured, such as the spelling of the English words 'ice' and 'queen' (previously 'is' and 'cwen') (Sampson, 1985).

Latin also had an important influence on English spelling. Latin spelling, which, pre-conquest, had been quite distinct from English spelling and had even been written in a different script, was now drawn on by the Normans, particularly in the spelling of French words that were relatively close to their Latin origins. For example, words with an initial 'h' in Latin, but no such sound in French, had the 'h' re-introduced in their spelling. This is how we get words such as 'honour' and 'hour'. So by the end of the 11th century, English spelling had become an amalgam of two major sets of rules, and a third one relating to pronunciation of another language. It is not surprising, then, that in medieval England a number of different spellings were considered acceptable for a given word. With the introduction of printing in the 15th century, this diversity became an advantage as compositors could choose the spellings that best fitted the spaces available.

But of course English spelling did not reach its present complexity until well after the Norman Conquest. Printing made another contribution. The first compositors, who came from Holland with Caxton, brought with them the spelling conventions of the Low Countries, giving us words such as 'ghost'. In the early 16th century, the French fashion for etymological spellings swept England, giving us spellings such as 'debt', 'salmon', 'corpse' and 'sceptre' for 'dette', 'samon' and 'cors' and 'septre'. In some cases (such as 'corpse', for example), changes to pronunciation appear to have followed the spelling changes. Some standardized spellings, such as 'foreign', were founded on error – in this case the mistaken idea that the word relates to 'reign', when it actually derives from the Old French 'forain', or the Latin 'foranum'.

This departure from the phonographic principle, this move away from transparency, came at a particularly significant time, for in the late 16th century, printers began to move to a fixed spelling for each word, a process that was completed by about 1650, since when there have been few changes. However, many words have since been imported from other languages, often with the spelling conventions of their country of origin. Words such as 'blitz' and 'chauffeur' bring with them rather different spelling patterns.

Meanwhile, the pronunciation of polysyllabic words, such as 'woman', 'station', 'develop', 'arrange' and 'composition', involves stress on alternate syllables, with the unstressed vowels (for example, the 'a' in 'woman') transforming into the sound known to linguists by the German name 'schwa'. However, the original vowel letter is retained in the spelling. In a similar way, the spelling of the past-tense suffix on the end of verbs such as 'marked', 'jumped and 'landed' remains constant, while the pronunciations of it differ.

We are so used to thinking of these '-ed's as telling us the same information, that we may not be aware that they actually represent three distinct syllables in these three words. Try saying them out loud. This is true also of the plural 's' in 'frogs' and 'ships'.

All these examples show a drift away from the phonographic principle towards a representation that is more morphological – more based on the meaning of root words and key suffixes, rather than a strict representation of their pronunciation on a phoneme-by-phoneme basis. This has its advantages: in their written form we can clearly see the link between 'compose' and 'composition' that is masked in pronunciation.

This brief canter through the history of English orthography might seem a distraction from the spelling patterns young children have to learn, but it is important to recognize that English spelling is neither straightforwardly transparent, nor chaotically opaque. There are patterns and regularities, even if these are more complex than for most other alphabetic languages.

The patterns of English orthography

This potted history of English spelling has shown many different systems at work. We don't need to teach young children the history (although parts of it may well interest them). But we do need to help them become aware of the systems at work in the words they encounter when learning to read and to spell. Children need to have control of these systems, in recognizing their key features, if they are to become 'self-teaching', learning new words for themselves.

The first key feature is as stated earlier. *At base the English writing system works by representing phonemes with graphemes.* But to make them independent decoders, it is never going to be enough to teach children the phoneme–grapheme correspondences of words such as 'dog' and 'cat', whose spellings remain relatively close to their Old English origins. We need to help them become aware of other patterns. Rhyme is particularly useful here: in groups such as 'dance' and 'glance', 'ball' and 'call' the words both rhyme and have the same end spellings: in each set, the *rime* – the part from the vowel to the end of the word – is identical. The rime is a stable spelling that represents a stable pronunciation, and so provides a better clue to word identification than does a grapheme-by-grapheme analysis. So we've come to the second key feature of English orthography: rime patterns. *The rime is often a more reliable guide to pronunciation than are the individual letters that go to make it up.*

One important reason for this is often overlooked. In contrast with Spanish, Italian and Finnish, all of which, as we have seen, have a more phonographic orthography, English is vowel rich. Leaving aside those gliding vowels, the diphthongs, Spanish has only five simple vowels, each of which is represented

-ack	-ain	-ake	-ale	-all	-ame	-an	-ank
-ap	-ash	-at	-ate	-aw	-ay	-eat	-ell
-est	-ice	-ick	-ide	-ite	-ill	-in	-ine
-ing	-ink	-ip	-ir	-ock	-oke	-op	-or
-ore	-uck	-ug	-ump	-unk			

Table 8.1   Thirty-seven rimes that yield nearly 500 words in English (Wylie and Durell, 1970: 787–91)

by a separate letter, whereas English has 12 vowel phonemes. But of course we don't have 12 vowel letters. Graphemes made up of two vowel letters extend the range somewhat, giving us words such as 'team', 'street' and 'goat'. But it's frequently the consonant (or consonant combination) following the vowel letter that determines its pronunciation. It's the 'st' in 'most' that shows how the 'o' is pronounced. Similarly, the letter 'a' represents three different phonemes in the words 'cat', 'call', and 'cast'. The pattern holds for 'fat', 'fall' and 'fast'. The reasons for this are explained in more detail in Chapter 6.

Attention to the onset and the rime are much more likely to yield something approaching an acceptable pronunciation for a word such as 'stall' or 'stake' than sounding it out grapheme by grapheme. Table 8.1 shows how productive this is in English.

There are similar patterns in two-syllable words, and even patterns that operate between the rime patterns. We don't need an etymological dictionary to see all of these patterns: words such as 'little', 'nettle', 'battle' and 'bottle' clearly go together, with connections to others such as 'puddle' and 'apple'. Having learned to recognize or spell one group, children are well placed to learn the others by analogy. In this way, armed with the alphabetic principle and an awareness of such spelling patterns, children can 'bootstrap' their way identifying new words for themselves.

There is one final set of patterns that can help children gain control over English orthography and see it as something other than chaotically arbitrary. These are the patterns based on the morphemic principle, where the spelling of a word indicates its meaning more clearly than its pronunciation, as in words such as 'southern'. This then, can be said to be the third key feature of English orthography. *The spelling of a word may tell us as much or more about its meaning as it does about its pronunciation.*

And finally, we have to admit that the complex history of English orthography has resulted in a number of quite idiosyncratic spellings. There are indeed many English spellings ('two', 'many', 'friends') that can't be easily marshalled into recognizable and predictable patterns.

The 20 most common words in English, in order of frequency:

| the | of | and | a | to | in | is | you | that | it |
| he | for | was | on | are | as | with | his | they | at |

The next 30 most common words:

be	this	from	I	have	or	by	one	had	not
but	what	all	were	when	we	there	can	an	your
which	there	said	if	do	will	each	about	how	up

And the next 50 most common words:

out	them	then	she	many	some	so	these	would	other
into	has	more	her	two	like	him	see	time	could
no	make	than	first	been	its	who	now	people	my
made	over	did	down	only	way	find	use	may	water
long	little	very	after	words	called	just	where	most	know

Table 8.2   **The 100 most common words in written English (Carroll et al., 1971)**

Can't we just start children off with the easiest words?

Starting children off with the 'easiest words' is what many phonics schemes have tried to do over the decades. Starting children off with words such as 'bat' and 'cat', 'man' and 'pan', with a straightforward one-to-one relationship between phonemes and letters, demonstrates the alphabetic principle. But it's very hard to make a readable text without words such as 'a', 'the', 'I' and 'you'. The harsh fact is that it's the commonest words in the English language which have the most irregular spellings; Table 8.2 shows this clearly.

Although this list is from the United States and is 25 years old, it is accepted as having a continued relevance for us in the United Kingdom. Looking at these lists, we can see that it would be hard to construct even a simple text for young children learning to read without using a number of these words. To read a range of texts with any degree of fluency and accuracy – such as that required to demonstrate a Level 2 in England's national curriculum (the notional level for a 7-year-old) – a child would have to be able to recognize all these words.

● Words with totally transparent one-to-one phoneme–letter relationships

So how can we rate the transparency of the spellings in the 100 commonest words in written English? Start by taking the ideal notion of a one-to-one correspondence between phonemes and letters, and go through the first 20 words on this list to find how many meet this criterion, making sure you pronounce the words in an unforced way, as you would in conversation. Highlight these 'totally transparent' words. Do the same with the next 30 and the same again with the last 50.

Only 5 of the first 20 words on this list can really be said to be 'transparent', leaving 15 spellings that are less than transparent. Of the next 30, 9 are transparent, leaving 21 non-transparent spellings. With the next 50 the ratio gets slightly worse: only 5 of them can be said to have a fully transparent spelling, leaving 45 non-transparent spellings. If you have highlighted more than 19 words, check them again carefully. *Out of the 100 words most used in written English, 81 fail to meet the test of fully transparent spellings, where one letter consistently represents one phoneme.*

● Words with two-letter graphemes consistently representing single phonemes

Now try highlighting (perhaps in another colour) words in which common two-letter graphemes, such as 'ee', 'th' and 'ow', are used to represent single phonemes. Count your results. By this means your tally of non-transparent spellings (those still not highlighted) should have dropped to 12 for the first 20, 17 for the next 30 and 32 for the next 50, making 61 in all. Check again if you come up with different figures. But we're already bending the rules slightly: the 'th' grapheme is used to represent two different phonemes: the sound at the beginning of 'the' and the one at the end of 'with' are really quite distinct.

We certainly can't stretch the rules to count 'where' as a regular spelling of this sort, since the 'wh' grapheme in 'where' actually stands for two phonemes, which would more accurately be represented as 'hw'. And in 'who', it stands for something closer to the 'h' in 'hat', whereas in most pronunciations of 'which' it stands for something more like the 'w' in 'wet'. *So out of the 100 commonest words, 61 cannot be regarded as orthographically transparent.*

These are words that can't simply be 'sounded out' one letter, or even one grapheme, at a time. This has a profound implication for the teaching of phonics. If we are not to confine children to artificial texts with a restricted range of words, our phonics teaching has to reflect other patterns in addition to the one-to-one phoneme–grapheme correspondences of the 'c-a-t' or 'ch-i-p' variety.

● Sets of words sharing rimes and rhymes

Highlight (in a third colour) and list the words from Figure 8.2 in rhyming groups. You can do these between sections, as well as within them, grouping 'to' with 'do', for example. Make sure you are pronouncing the words in an unforced way when you make your judgements. As you will have found, there are patterns in these 61 less-than-totally transparent spellings. We can see and hear that 'to', 'do' and 'who' go together, as do 'no' and 'so', and 'is' and 'his', and 'as' and 'has'. Then 'he', 'be', 'we' and 'she', 'would' and 'could', 'there' and 'where' (but not 'were') form similar patterns. How many other groupings of this sort can you find, both between words on the list, and also between them and other words in common use?

● Patterns in the remaining words

Look at the words still not highlighted. Can you see any other patterns at work? You may find one or two, but there is no escaping the fact that most of these have to be learned as 'sight' words, and as singletons, at least initially. If children are to have texts that are not totally artificial, they will need to learn words such as 'was', 'you' and 'one'. Even the initial letters are not necessarily reliable, particularly if they are vowels. 'Sounding out' is unlikely to yield words such as 'other' or 'any'. This is the 'deep orthography' of English.

● Where does this leave us?

Teaching children to read in English is not the same as teaching them to read a transparent orthography such as Italian, Spanish, Finnish or Swahili. It is more complex. More patterns are involved and we need to be aware of this. And then there are the exceptions to the patterns. So we need to teach children not only the alphabetic principle, but also the other patterns that shape English orthography, particularly rhyme/rime patterns. And we also need to teach them those essential 'one-off' words.

Exactly when and how we do this is a matter of careful decision making about young children's capacity to learn different sets of patterns, their need for meaningful 'naturalistic' texts and their capacity to learn in different ways. But phonics teaching that is, consciously or otherwise, founded on the idea that English spelling is straightforwardly phonographic will not meet the requirement of teaching children to teach themselves the words they need to know to become effective readers of English.

SOMETHING TO THINK ABOUT

- Compare Dombey's argument (this chapter) concerning the deep orthography of English spelling to Huxford's argument (Chapter 7) concerning how we use phonics in the teaching of spelling. How do the authors agree? In what ways do they differ?

SOMETHING TO READ

If you are interested in exploring more about the complex history of the English language, try:

- Bryson, B. (1990) *Mother Tongue: The English language*. Harmondsworth: Penguin.
- Crystal, D. (2002) *The English Language*. Harmondsworth: Penguin.
- Bragg, M. (2004) *The Adventure of English*. London: Sceptre.

SOMETHING TO DO

- If you have not already done so, complete the activities relating to Table 8.2: The 100 most common words in the English language. Then select two or three popular books for young children. See how many of the words in the first few pages fit any of the patterns you have explored. Which are words that would need to be learned individually? What are the implications for reading such books for children using only a synthetic phonics approach?

Chapter 9

Sounds Familiar: The History of Phonics Teaching

Moya Cove

> There are many competing detailed methods each with its own supporters and detractors, but it is now generally recognized that no single method is applicable to all children on all occasions.

At first glance this comment from a government-initiated report on the teaching of reading looks as if it has come straight from the seminal Bullock Report of 1975, *A Language for Life*. It bears strong resemblance to one of Bullock's most celebrated conclusions, namely that 'There is no one method, medium, approach, device, or philosophy that holds the key to learning to read' (DES, 1975: 521). The above extract, however, is taken from a pamphlet entitled *Reading Ability: Some Suggestions for Helping the Backward* and was produced by a 1947 government committee in response to post-War concerns about the extent of school illiteracy among school leavers in England (Diack, 1965: 37).

One might be excused for wondering what happened in the intervening 28 years and why there was need in 1975 to give such a similar message, and why, indeed, these signposts from other times still have critical resonance for us today. These matters are, of course, far from straightforward, but the two quotations do serve to illustrate one of the most striking features of the history of phonics – and that is the number of commonalities, in the debates and theoretical positions, across the decades. How far these seemingly recurrent discourses have helped or hindered effective practice in the classroom is a question we might ask ourselves of the history, and constitutes at least part of the phonics debate at the beginning of the 21st century. This chapter offers an historical overview of the teaching of phonics in England and America and highlights, from the extensive literature, just some of the episodes which have shaped our thinking and practice in the teaching of phonics within early reading.

Teaching reading before the advent of phonic methods: the alphabet and the growth of the alphabetic method

The alphabets most commonly used throughout the world today are descended from the Phoenician alphabet developed during the 12th century BC. The Phoenician alphabet gradually developed from a pictographic form into a more abstract form of a phonetic, consonantal alphabet which was adopted by the Greeks and modified to include vowel representations. They became the first Europeans to write using an alphabet and, with the ensuing growth of modern European languages these alphabetic approaches dominated the teaching of reading from the Greek period to the 19th century.

The alphabetic method was centred on teaching children to recognize and name the letters of the alphabet, both capital and lower case, in alphabetical order. For the most part this was achieved through progressing from the alphabet to spelling out and saying the words of the bible. Diack reports that in 1846 one of Her Majesty's Inspectors commented that the '. . . sole text for all reading instruction was the language of Scripture in the authorized version' (1965: 11). However, in his study of the development of reading pedagogy, Diack also refers to teaching materials which seem to have departed from dependence on the Bible. One such example is the 'hornbook' developed in England in 1450, which comprised one sheet set in a wooden frame covered with transparent horn. It depicted the cross of Christ, the alphabet – in small and capital letters – and columns of *ab*, *eb* and *ib* syllables. The existence of these syllables caused Diack to question whether it was possible to differentiate with precision between alphabetic and phonic methods since the vowel–consonant pairing in the hornbook would suggest a focus on learning sounds rather than mere letter names. The hornbook, then, might be seen to herald a move towards a phonic approach. Interestingly, hornbooks spawned the 'gingerbread method' in the 18th century, when letters were made into gingerbread in an effort to enliven the 'wearisome drill' and inspire children to learn their letters – an early version, perhaps, of alphabetti spaghetti!

The 18th century saw the publication in America of Noah Webster's 'Speller', one of the most popular texts in the history of teaching reading and selling 80 million copies during the century following its publication (Congdon, 1974). This might best be described as a forerunner of the reading 'primer' and, while it employed a predominately alphabetic approach to teaching reading, the logic and organization of the approach points towards the beginning of phonics methods and again highlights the intricacies involved in making absolute distinctions between reading methodologies that emphasize code above context – an issue that continues to exercise us today.

In contrast to the alphabetic method, which so dominated 'formal' reading education in the 18th century, is the glimpse we can gain from consideration of Morag Styles' absorbing account of women writing poetry in their own homes for their own children which she describes as '. . . the secret history of domestic literacy' (1997: 154). Styles illustrates this through the work of Jane Johnson, a mother writing in 1740s England who, through her inventive poetry, offered her children an alternative introduction to early reading steeped, as it was, in the warmth of sharing richly captivating texts – and being more akin to the kind of support for emergent and beginning readers we so readily advocate today.

Teaching reading in the 19th century: the phonic method makes an entrance

The alphabetic method continued well into the 19th century, but began to be replaced by a phonic approach around 1850 which quickly gained popularity in both England and America. In England, HMI endorsed the use of a new 'phonic method' when, during the 1840s, Battersea Training College introduced this approach into their training programme. The 'new' approach, as described by a college president of the time, involved learning the sound '. . . not by its common arbitrary name but by the sound which it has in composition'; he went on to explain that after working on combinations of letter sounds on a slate board a reading book was introduced but '. . . not until the child has a necessity of it in his further progress; it is then a relief and not a task' (Diack, 1965: 28). Phonics teaching was widely embraced and approaches such as the Dale method (Diack, 1965: 105), which was prevalent in England between the late 19th and early 20th centuries, helped popularize the approach. This method was highly systematic and, in essence, involved a range of 'pre-reading' perceptual activities, introduction of letters and the fusion of separate sounds into words – all hallmarks of established practice at that time.

Publishers were not slow to exploit the opportunities presented through the new phonic method, and a number of books designed to help children grasp 'sounding out' began to appear. Hunter Diack reports on young Master Winston Churchill's experience (around 1880) with one such book published in 1857, *Reading Without Tears, A Pleasant Mode of Learning to Read*, and cites this revealing quote from Churchill's autobiography *My Early Life*: 'Mrs. Everest produced a book called *Reading Without Tears*. It certainly did not justify its title in my case. I was made aware that before the Governess arrived I must be able to read without tears. We toiled each day. My nurse pointed with a pen at the different letters. I thought it all very tiresome' (Diack, 1965: 30). How many children over a hundred-year period, we might ask ourselves, identified with Churchill's heartfelt recollections?

It might be tempting to believe, as we have perhaps sometimes assumed in recent decades, that those teachers who subscribed to the phonics approach did so as their sole method of instruction. However, practice in the mid-19th century, such as that revealed by Hilary Minns' study of Derby's poor schools and their work with Irish immigrant children, seems to dispel such notions. Evidence from the work of these schools, under the auspices of the Sisters of Mercy, appears to unearth a *mixture* of techniques, including 'alphabetical and synthesizing' methods (Minns, 1997). Minns reports that the overall approach to teaching reading was firmly child-centred and describes it as a catechetical method which gave '. . . high priority to understanding the meaning of words and sentences' through careful questioning (1997: 182). This practice points ahead to the 20th century where phonics is seen to take a more supporting role, albeit essential, within the whole reading process – rather than the exclusive role of the single method approach. Moreover, close scrutiny of the history of pedagogical perspectives and practices in the development of early reading shows that the Sisters of Mercy in Derby were not alone in their meaning-emphasis approach.

In America historical accounts of teaching reading show that between 1890 and 1920 a phonic system, where children were '. . . started out immediately with practice on sounds of isolated letters and family words' was the favoured method. Nila Smith, writing about this in the 1960s, described the approach as an 'elaborate synthetic system', and by the mid-20th century approaches resembling this method had become firmly established. One such example, Rebecca Pollard's 'Synthetic method of reading and spelling', which involved successive recognition and sounding of letter after letter to build up words, was widely used. In his extensive examination of specific systems for teaching reading, the psychologist Edmund Burke Huey was critical of Pollard's method; in particular, he questioned her view that there should be 'no guesswork, no reference to pictures and no waiting for a story from the teacher to develop children's thinking' (Diack, 1965: 50). Huey went on to influence significant changes to practice in America with his advocacy of word methods.

Teaching reading in the first half of the 20th century: phonics reframed within newer thinking on reading development

As advances in the understanding of the development of reading informed practice, the early part of the 20th century saw a changing scene. Nila Smith's (1963) review of practice in America shows that between 1920 and 1935 the phonic method fell out of favour as more emphasis was placed on silent reading to '. . . get the thought' (Chall, 1967: 161), but between 1920 and 1935 phonic methods were revived. The major shift, both in Britain and America, came with a move to the word, or 'look-and-say', method. This was promoted in America by Huey from 1908 onwards, and became well established in England during the 1940s through the influence of Gestalt learning theory and its consequent impact on reading theory. This resulted in treating whole words as basic learning units.

Chall reported on a period of relative consensus on methodology in America from about 1930 and details a set of eight principles on which effective pedagogy was founded from the 1930s to the 1960s. The statement on phonics specified that 'Drill or practice in phonics should be avoided; instead phonics should be "integrated" with meaningful connected reading. In addition, the child should not isolate sounds and blend them to form words. Instead he should identify unknown words through a process of visual analysis and substitution' (Chall, 1967: 14). This desire for balance (similarly advanced in the 1947 English pamphlet referred to at the beginning of the chapter) resonates across the decades to the present day.

Teaching reading in the second half of the 20th century: phonics, politics and positioning

Word methods continued to prevail until the mid-1950s, when the efficacy of the approach was called into question. In England, disquiet was expressed when a number of reading surveys highlighted that 'failing' readers lacked phonic knowledge, which generated considerable concern about children who were unable to read. In America the publication of *Why Johnny Can't Read* (Flesch, 1955), in the form of a letter from the mother of a child who had found reading difficult, caused an unprecedented public debate. Flesch's vehement criticism of word methods caused a significant backlash for the approach and brought calls for a return to phonics. Public unease was intensified when America suffered the space-race humiliation of Russia launching the first satellite in 1957, causing the Americans to look critically at their education system. In the aftermath, Jeanne Chall's *Learning to Read: The Great Debate* of 1967 explored reading pedagogy in detail and ultimately favoured phonic code methods. Chall found great diversity in the range of phonics programmes but concluded that they incorporated most of the conventional wisdom of the day with one major departure – the issue of pacing. The authors of the separate phonics programmes felt that phonics teaching through the basal readers was '. . . too little, too late' (Chall, 1967: 23), and their own published programmes reflected this with an earlier and more intensive emphasis on phonics.

In England, the impact of Flesch's book was not insignificant, particularly since public interest in developing a strong education system was acute in the post-War period. The teaching of reading became increasingly politicized in England and America and, with the growth of state education systems and educational research, there came a wider and more rigorous debate. Although the pendulum swung back to an emphasis on phonics, newer varieties of the method appeared, such as the phonic–word method developed by Daniels and Diack in the 1950s and reported by Southgate as '. . . an analytic approach to phonics in contrast with the older synthetic approaches … beginning with whole words which were contrasted with similar words and the differences analysed (Southgate and Roberts, 1970: 41). But while teachers now had a wider range of approaches to draw from, methodologies and teaching materials were still predominately code-based.

The groundbreaking Bullock report (DES) of 1975 helped to establish holistic, language experience approaches and encouraged the principle that reading, writing, talking and listening should be treated as a unity; moreover, the report stressed the vital role of the teacher (and the teacher's thorough understanding of the breadth of factors at work in the development of reading) as the most critical 'resource' in the teaching of reading. The message on the importance of a balanced 'eclectic' approach was accentuated and, as new insights into reading development transpired from emergent literacy theory (Holdaway, 1979; Hall, 1987), the period into the 1980s saw many practice shifts into whole language techniques.

However, the 1980s also saw increasing polarization of practitioners through their alignment with either a code or a meaning emphasis on the teaching of early reading. This was most notable through the growth of the 'real books' approach (Waterland, 1985) where the emphasis on decoding artificially constructed texts was challenged and real reading experiences, using real books, was promoted. David Wray, writing in 1989, refers to the upholders of 'bottom-up' and 'top-down' positions as actors in 'The New Debate', and contrasts this with the issues in Chall's 'Great Debate' – he draws the distinction between the 1967 debate, which centred on the relative merits of code versus code methods, and the 1980s debate, which centred on the relative merits of meaning versus code methods in the teaching of reading.

Entrenchment of positions remained a feature of the practice scene until the research on phonemic awareness and phonological processing (pioneered by the work of Peter Bryant, Usha Goswami and Lynette Bradley in the early 1980s), began to impact on policy, practice and reading schemes in the late 1980s and early 1990s. This research, discussed elsewhere in this book, brought about a watershed in the treatment of phonics, with the stress on teaching phonic knowledge *within* the reading process. This reframing of phonics, described by Nicholas Bielby in *Making Sense of Reading* (1994) as the 'new phonics', led to a greater focus on phonological processing and widespread uptake of what has been termed, in a catch-all way, 'analytic phonics'. Bielby presses home the distinctions between 'traditional' and 'new' phonics and is emphatic that the updated rationale for phonics teaching should not be confused with the 'first and fast' approach associated with early rote drills.

From the late 1990s, as analytic phonics became widely practised and a balanced approach was further endorsed within the National Literacy Strategy's Searchlights Model, a period of relative harmony ensued. This period, however, was to be short-lived. The emergence of Johnston and Watson's research evidence from Clackmannanshire (SOEID, 1998) on the success of children taught to read using synthetic phonics opened up a renewed focus on how phonics was taught; the Clackmannanshire findings set in motion a chain of events which included a national review of the teaching of phonics in England and which culminated with the publication of the Rose Report (DfES, 2005a). This most recent chapter in the history of teaching phonics is well documented elsewhere in this book, but suffice it to say here that there may well appear to be echoes of earlier history resounding in 2006.

Teaching reading in the 21st century: what now for phonics?

Looking at the history of the teaching of phonics brings about a distinct sense of déjà vu, and the unhelpful phonics dichotomy could so easily lead to a state of confusion for the class teacher whose prime objective is to support reading development in the most effective way possible. The more contested issues – of what form of phonics approach to use, how systematic it should be, when to start it and how fast to pace it – run through the history as familiar leitmotivs. But at the same time the history shows that, from as early as the 18th century, there have been champions of reading for meaning and mixed-teaching methods.

The evidence on how the most effective teachers of literacy support reading development (Medwell et al., 1998) yields important insights with regard to teaching phonics, most notably that they place an emphasis on '. . . embedding systematic attention to word and sentence level aspects of reading and writing within whole text activities which are both meaningful and explained clearly to pupils' (1998: 31). Moreover, the effective teachers studied by Medwell and her colleagues were found to have '. . . developed a variety of coherent theoretical positions and were able to synthesize these into a working philosophy which underpinned their teaching' (1998: 66). The importance of this kind of informed belief system has been pointed out many times (Diack, 1965; Southgate and Roberts, 1970; Bullock in DES, 1975) and is reinforced most recently in the United Kingdom Literacy Association *Submission to the Review of Best Practice in the Teaching of Early Reading* where the 'profound role' of the teacher is once again highlighted (UKLA, 2005).

The question Chall posed in the 1960s of 'Why don't we learn from the past?' (1967: 93) still seems apposite today, and one that we must surely address if we are to avoid phonics history repeating itself. The key recommendations in the UKLA submission to the review of best practice suggest that we need neither an allegiance to one or other phonics approach or new teaching materials but, rather, we should enhance the quality of implementation of existing programmes. It would be heartening to be able to report in years to come that this had been harmoniously achieved, but given that the history shows an outbreak of phonics panic every ten years or so (with uncanny proximity to the mid-decade point), perhaps we should all watch this space in 2015!

SOMETHING TO THINK ABOUT

- 'Why don't we learn from the past?' (Chall, 1967: 93): discuss with colleagues why the debates around phonics are still so fierce today. What would help teachers to move forward and avoid yet more polarization of thinking and practice?
- 'What is right at one level of teaching reading may be insufficient at another . . . and wrong at yet another. Furthermore, the question of teaching reading is not a question of teaching either this way or that way, but in most cases teaching both this way and that way' (Jansen, 1985: 172): what are the implications of this in relation to the teacher's role in teaching phonics and in supporting children's reading development?

SOMETHING TO READ

- Jeanne Chall reviewed and evaluated hundreds of research studies on reading covering the period 1910 to 1965, and in addition visited classrooms and interviewed teachers and textbook publishers. Sifting the literature took Chall three years, writing up her conclusions took a further two. *Learning to Read: The Great Debate* (1967) is an important book available from most university libraries, or summaries are easily found on the Internet. It is interesting to see in what ways the debate remains the same and in what ways it has changed since 1967.

SOMETHING TO DO

- Collect examples of beginning reading books written in decodable text, which use only words that display a direct phoneme-to-grapheme correspondence. Compare them to beginning reading books that do not have this characteristic. Consider the advantages/disadvantages of each type of book for readers.
- Ask children and adults who are confident, competent readers to reflect on the support they received to use decoding strategies when they were beginning readers. Can they remember, for example, what worked for them or what struggles they encountered along the way? Can these insights inform our practice?

Chapter 10

Responses to Rose: The Final Report of the Independent Review of the Teaching of Early Reading

Maureen Lewis and Sue Ellis

In this chapter, educationalists with differing views on the best way to teach reading give their response to the final report of the review into the teaching of reading, undertaken by Jim Rose on behalf of the Department for Education (DfES, 2006). Although not statutory, this report will guide future policy on the teaching of reading in England. Its recommendations are of considerable significance to that country and may have a wider impact as a model for those in other countries who wish to see more attention given to the teaching of phonics.

The Road to the Rose Review

Maureen Lewis and Sue Ellis

The setting up of the Rose Review was the culmination of a campaign over several years by pressure groups and individuals who believed that the multi-strategy approach (including phonics) advocated by the National Literacy Strategy/Primary National Strategy was ineffective. They believed that the model of phonics teaching offered by the NLS was flawed. Some of these critics argued that an explicit 'synthetic phonics first and only' approach would be more successful in teaching children to read. The introduction to this book gives a detailed outline of these debates. At the same time as some critics were arguing for more phonics teaching, others argued for a return to a less structured (or regimented, as they saw it) approach to literacy teaching with a greater emphasis on reading for enjoyment and reading quality books.

In the years from 2000, many parliamentary questions relating to synthetic phonics were asked, mainly by a small group of Conservative Party MPs (see Hansard website), and newspapers printed articles asking why there was not more phonics teaching in schools. In 2003, in response to what appeared to be a concerted campaign in parliament and the media, and following the publication of *Teaching of Phonics in Primary Schools* (Ofsted, 2001), the DfES held an invitation seminar on phonics teaching. Advocates of a synthetic phonics 'only and early' approach were represented at the seminar, as were authors of a range of phonics programmes, phonics experts from the research community and representatives of the NLS. The papers from this seminar are available online at http://www.standards.dfes.gov.uk/primary/publications/literacy/686807/

In response to this seminar, the National Literacy Strategy slightly amended its advice on the pace and sequence for teaching phonics and produced new support materials, *Playing with Sounds* (DfES, 2003a). It advocated both synthetic and analytic phonics and re-emphasized the importance of regular, systematic teaching of phonemic awareness skills and phonics from foundation stage onwards. Nevertheless, debate on the best way to teach beginning readers continued in the press and in parliament. In 2004, the House of Commons Education and Skills Select Committee set up a parliamentary inquiry to investigate 'the methods used in schools to teach children to read':

> We took evidence from witnesses who argued that 'phonics' programmes should have more prominence in the early teaching of reading (these programmes concentrate on establishing an early understanding of sound–letter correspondence). We took evidence from others who questioned the utility of this approach, preferring to focus on the development of vocabulary and the enrichment of linguistic experience, as well as from those who support the current Government advice in the form of the Primary National Strategy. Many of those who contacted us during this inquiry argued passionately for or against these different methods. Our aim was to determine objectively which method worked best, based on the available evidence, or, if the evidence was insufficient, to recommend steps that should be taken in order to reach a conclusion. (House of Commons Education and Skills Committee, 2005: para. 3)

After an inquiry lasting several months, the committee came to no definitive conclusion but recommended that:

> In view of the evidence from the Clackmannanshire study, as well as evidence from other schools where synthetic phonics programmes have been introduced, we recommend that the Government should undertake an immediate review of the National Literacy Strategy. This should determine whether the current prescriptions and recommendations are the best available methodology for the teaching of reading in primary schools... We strongly urge the DfES to commission a large-scale comparative study, comparing the National Literacy Strategy with 'phonics fast and first' approaches. (House of Commons Education and Skills Committee, 2005: para. 52)

As a result of these recommendations, in June 2005 the DfES appointed Jim Rose (the former HMI, Director of Inspection at Ofsted) and a panel of advisers, most of whom had a background in psychological research, to 'examine current evidence about practices for teaching children to read to ensure that the Strategy can continue to provide the most effective support for assuring children's progression in reading' (DfES, 2005a).

The 'Rose Review', as it became known, was charged with examining five aspects:

1   What best practice should be expected in the teaching of early reading and synthetic phonics.
2   How this relates to the development of the birth-to-five framework (now known as the Early Years Foundation Stage) and the development and renewal of the National Literacy Strategy *Framework for Teaching*.
3   What range of provision best supports children with significant literacy difficulties and enables them to catch up with their peers, and the relationship of such targeted intervention programmes with synthetic phonics teaching.
4   How leadership and management in schools can support the teaching of reading, as well as practitioners' subject knowledge.
5   The value for money or cost-effectiveness of the range of approaches the review considers.

In giving the committee this remit, the DfES also made clear that as phonics was 'already a central part of the approaches recommended by the Primary National Strategy', the issue for the review was 'not whether to teach phonics, but how' (DfES, 2005a).

Recommendations of the final report

The interim report was published in November 2005 and the final report was published in March 2006. The final report recommends that:

●   In relation to aspect 1 (best practice in teaching phonics)

–   Priority and clear guidance should be given to developing children's speaking and listening skills.
–   High-quality, systematic phonic work as defined by the review should be taught discretely as the prime approach in learning to decode (to read) and encode (to write/spell) print.
–   Phonic work should be set within a broad and rich language curriculum.
–   The Primary National Strategy should continue to exemplify the kind of teaching all children should experience (quality-first teaching).

●   In relation to aspect 2 (early years, foundation stage and renewal of the NLS framework)

–   For most children, high-quality, systematic phonic work should start by the age of five. This should be multi-sensory.

- The Searchlight model of reading should be reconstructed.
- The early years, foundation stage and the renewed literacy framework must be compatible with each other and give guidance on continuity and progression in phonic work.

● In relation to aspect 3 (supporting children with significant literacy difficulties)

- High-quality phonic work should be a priority within normal classroom teaching.
- Additional support should be compatible with mainstream practice.
- Interventions should be matched to the different types of special educational needs.

● In relation to aspect 4 (leadership and management and practitioners' subject knowledge and skills)

- Leaders should make sure that phonic work is given appropriate priority in the teaching of beginner readers.
- At least one member of staff should be fully able to lead on literacy, especially phonic work.
- Leaders should monitor the quality and consistency of phonic work and give staff feedback.

The report also recommends a series of additional training and professional development opportunities to increase teacher, trainee and teaching assistant knowledge about early reading, particularly phonics (aspect 5).

Practioners, teacher associations and literacy associations have welcomed some of these recommendations. Others are more controversial. This range of reactions is reflected in the response pieces that follow.

A Rose is a Rows: a Celebration of the Importance of Accurate Word Reading to Ensure Understanding of Texts

Rhona Stainthorp

'What do you think of the Rose Review, . . . in 500 words, . . . by the end of the month?' said the e-mail. Since we're talking here of the *Independent Review of the Teaching of Early Reading* (DfES, 2006a), it is clear that, indeed, a rose by any other name would smell as sweet: this report will always be known as the Rose Review. Any other independent chairperson and there may have been no pleasing alliteration. No shared initial phonemes and, as we all know, awareness of phonemes really is useful for mapping letter–sound correspondences. And mapping letter–sound correspondences is essential for achieving the alphabetic principle, thus paving the way for accurate word reading. Under different guidance we might not have had such a wise and thoughtful report. And, as in so many other areas, Shakespeare got there first:

> *Servant*:   . . . but, I pray, can you read anything you see?
> *Romeo*:   Ay, if I know the letters and the language.

> Romeo and Juliet: Act 1, Scene II

It took Gough and Tumner (1986) another 400 years or so to come up with the 'simple view of reading'. But better late than never.

There are many positive aspects of the Review, but I want to focus on the decision to steer the teaching of reading away from its predication on the 'searchlights model' towards a recognition that reading is the product of accurate word reading and language comprehension. As is made explicit in the appendix to the review, there is clear empirical evidence that skilled readers are accurate, fast, effortless word readers but poor readers are slow, laborious and often inaccurate. Beginner readers also find word reading challenging. However, if they are taught the letter–sound correspondences and how to blend sounds into words, they are armed with a strategy for reading words independently. No one argues that this will produce 100 per cent accuracy in English as would be the case in a transparent orthography like Turkish. However, if children have this knowledge they have a necessary tool for developing fluent word reading. The searchlights analogy was a distraction because it proposed that the four searchlights were equally useful and interchangeable. The Review has accepted that this is not the case. In acknowledging the 'simple view of reading' as a more accurate account, the importance of language comprehension for reading has also been highlighted.

Quite rightly, the report recognizes that there are teacher education implications if the recommendations for teaching early reading are to feed forward to better school achievement. Initial teacher education will have to move from 'this is what to do and how to do it' towards 'this is why you should do it and here is the literature with the empirical evidence to back this up'. This throws the ball squarely into the universities' court to guide students through the research evidence.

The review is not a nice knock-down argument, but it is a knockout. It's a genuinely thoughtful, measured document that deserves to be read in full. It should form the basis of university seminars and school inservice sessions on the teaching of reading.

And don't forget to read the appendix – 'there's glory for you'. Well, she would say that, wouldn't she!

Editors' note: Rhona Stainthorp was one of the authors of the appendix to the Rose Review.

Getting Phonics into Perspective

Jennifer Chew, on Behalf of the Reading Reform Foundation

The Reading Reform Foundation (RRF) welcomes the Rose Review, which deals clearly and fairly with important issues.

The searchlights model

Most important of all is the way that it deals with the 'searchlights' model which was at the heart of the original National Literacy Strategy (NLS) *Framework for Teaching* (DfEE, 1998a). This model, based on views which had been strongly held in Britain since at least the early 1980s, proposed that children should, from the very beginning of learning to read, identify printed words by using not only grapheme-phoneme knowledge but also grammatical knowledge, contextual knowledge and the recognition of whole words. As the Rose Review says, however, 'a model of reading which encourages switching between various searchlight strategies, particularly when phonic work is regarded as only one such strategy, all of equal worth, risks paying insufficient attention to the critical skills of word recognition which must first be secured by beginner readers' (DfES, 2006: para. 116). A similar comment from an Ofsted report is quoted in para. 118. The RRF has always opposed the searchlights model and welcomes the scholarly account of the real relationship between 'word recognition' and 'language comprehension' which is given in Appendix 1 of the Rose Review.

Blending

The Rose Review notes that 'nearly half the schools visited did not give enough time to teaching children the crucial skill of blending (synthesizing) sounds together' (DfES, 2006: para. 232). This is probably a consequence of the searchlights model: blending is an important part of phonic decoding, but the need to teach it is obscured when other ways of identifying words are seen as being as valid as phonic decoding. Synthetic phonics, which the RRF has always supported, teaches beginners to use phonic decoding as their only means of identifying words in reading, and therefore teaches them not only how to produce sounds for graphemes from left to right all through each word, but also how to blend these sounds together. It should be easier for teachers to understand the need for this once they have understood the Rose Review's criticism of the searchlights model, and once they realize that Rose is also right to say that learning to decode phonically can be rewarding and stimulating for beginners. This approach also allows the reversibility of reading and spelling to be stressed much more than is possible with a multiple-cueing approach to reading. Related to this is the matter of decodable texts: the Rose Review does not come down firmly in favour of these, but it allows that there may be a place for them (they can enable children to benefit from 'quick wins' and gain confidence – 2006: para. 82) and it makes the point that decodable books of good quality are now available. Allowing children to practise on these books does not preclude the reading aloud of more advanced books by teachers.

Research and common sense

Where directly applicable research findings were felt to be inconclusive, the Rose team decided that observation based on common sense was a reasonable guide. The RRF agrees, and would point out that research findings might have been more conclusive if more rigorous studies had been carried out by government departments and/or by others who have argued against a pure synthetic phonics approach for beginners. The NLS, which we have had since 1998, has itself not been based on rigorous research, as is clear from Appendix 1 of the Rose Review. While the research cited in this Appendix may not provide clear evidence that synthetic phonics is better than analytic phonics, it *does* provide justification for the abandoning of the searchlights model. From this point of view, the way forward that the Rose Review proposes is more research-based than the multiple-cueing approach, which has been officially sanctioned since 1998 and which was widely promoted in Britain for many years before that.

Conclusion

The RRF believes that the Rose Review provides the rationale for an approach to literacy teaching which is not only scientifically sound but also lively and stimulating for children. This approach, if properly implemented, should raise reading and spelling standards significantly and quickly.

Keeping Phonics in Perspective

John Stannard

The Rose Review presents a sensible appraisal of the teaching of early reading. It reiterates advice the NLS has been giving since 1998, reinforced with evidence from more recent research. He doesn't much like the 'searchlights' and wants it replaced with Morag Stuart's and Rhona Stainthorp's 'dual-route' model (see Appendix 1, The Rose Review). They posit a 'simple' account of reading in which word recognition and comprehension are distinct but parallel *components, dimensions* or *processes* which, they argue, must exist separately because they can be more or less separately described. The model is used to imply that the reading curriculum should consist of two parallel but distinct streams designed to develop these allegedly distinct psychological processes. Although the model is heavy with presupposition, Rose's conclusions still make a lot of sense. On the one hand he wants to see early, focused and fast teaching of phonics, or to paraphrase:

> At Key Stage 1, there should be a strong and systematic emphasis on the teaching of phonics . . . pupils should be taught to:
>
> - discriminate between the separate sounds in words;
> - learn the letters and letter combinations most commonly used to spell those sounds;
> - read words by sounding out and blending their separate parts;
> - write words by combining the spelling patterns of their sounds. (DfEE, 1998a: 4)

But this description is taken not from the Review but from the introductory text in the NLS *Framework for Teaching* explaining the diagram of the searchlights metaphor.

In parallel, Rose argues that there should be a rich experience of books and reading and a renewed emphasis on speaking and listening, to develop positive attitudes, vocabulary and communication skills. Route 1 sounds like *Progression in Phonics* (DfEE, 1999a) or *Jolly Phonics* (Lloyd and Jolly, 1995) plus carefully levelled texts, while route 2 is more like shared reading and story telling. In time these two 'routes' should fuse into one, though it is not entirely clear how this is supposed to occur.

The searchlights metaphor does not make this hard-and-fast distinction, but applies different emphases at different stages of reading. In the early stages, children should use phonics as a first strategy for decoding. If they cannot decode a word phonically, they should use other knowledge to help work it out, then check it back; if they decode a word but don't understand it, they should try to derive its meaning from the text and, if the text is predictable, they should use its momentum to accelerate the decoding of words. Critics don't much like this because they think it confuses children.* But this is opinion, not fact. While we know that phonics improves decoding, there is no evidence that, where children are taught phonics systematically, using other strategies to make sense of texts confuses them. On the contrary, it is how most successful readers learn. Far from 'guessing' at words, as it is sometimes pejoratively described, they learn to predict, make sense, create connections, self-correct and build autonomy. This strengthens rather than diminishes the importance of phonics as the first line of attack on words, and underlines the value of teaching it early, systematically and rapidly.

We should get this into perspective. For teachers, nothing much hangs on which metaphor or model is preferred, provided we are clear about what strategies work in practice, and allow reasonable latitude for teachers to differentiate and apply them wisely. Rose has set this out pretty well, bearing in mind the sensitivities of the various lobbies, and aligned his advice carefully with the NLS. The much-vaunted Clackmannanshire study (Johnston and Watson, 2005), if it shows anything, shows that good phonics teaching delivers reading accuracy and fluency but has little impact on comprehension.

In 2005, 84 per cent of year 6 children in England achieved level 4 in national tests for reading and more than 90 per cent achieved level 3. These scores could go down. Getting more children to level 4 (the expected level for 11-year-olds) means improving the performance of level 3s, who already '. . . read a range of texts fluently and accurately [and] read independently, using strategies appropriately to establish meaning' (English National Curriculum Statutory Order, Level 3 description, DfES and QCA, 2000). Improvement depends more on teaching comprehension and even more on the effective teaching of writing. Sadly, neither of these was within Jim Rose's remit, and I doubt that mandating phonics in the National Curriculum or investing money in training teachers on the Stuart and Stainthorp model will make the necessary difference.

Editors' note: John Stannard, CBE, designed and directed the National Literacy Strategy from 1998 to 2003.

An Instructional Perspective on the Rose Review

Jonathan Solity

There are three issues that any approach to teaching literacy has to address. The first concerns the standards of lower-achieving pupils. It is generally

---

*See, for example, *Teaching Children to Read* (Education and Skills Committee, 2005), Report of the House of Commons Select Committee 21 March 2005, pp.13–14, where the Reading Reform Foundation and Ruth Miskin characterize it as 'contradictory', 'impossible', and a recipe for reinforcing failure.

recognized that approximately 20–25 per cent of pupils fail to reach acceptable levels at end of key stage 2, and that the majority of these children are from low-income families. This is a worrying state of affairs given the vast number of initiatives that successive governments have introduced to raise standards over the last 25 years.

The second issue concerns children's attitudes to reading. The evidence indicates that children in England are less positive about, and enjoy reading less, than their peers in comparable countries (Bell, 2005; PIRLS, 2001; Ofsted, 2004). The third issue concerns the extent to which progress has been made in implementing genuinely inclusive practices into schools. The NLS, through its three-wave model, effectively ensures that failing readers are excluded from mainstream classrooms and are withdrawn for additional one-to-one or small group help teaching.

The Rose Review skilfully addresses a range of issues and provides a starting point for addressing the above areas. Most notably it draws on research, where possible, to inform the advice offered. The Review is highly critical of the searchlights model; it was based on the flawed instructional premise that determining how to teach was best achieved through an analysis of experienced readers rather than a logical analysis of the skills required by beginning readers. Its withdrawal, given the dogma and vigour with which it was introduced, is the educational equivalent of Tony Blair acknowledging that there were never any weapons of mass destruction. The alternative framework focuses on decoding and comprehension. Carnine et al. (1997) provide a detailed analysis of their respective roles in teaching reading.

Rose recognizes the value of synthetic phonics, but notes the considerable differences between advocates of the approach. These are most obvious in relation to 'how much' phonics to teach and the role of reading schemes and real books. Gontijo et al. (2003) analysed 160,595 different words and found that they can be represented by 195 graphemes and 461 grapheme–phoneme associations. Solity and Vousden (2006) have shown that teaching as few as 60 grapheme–phoneme correspondences enable children to read the majority of monosyllabic words that they will encounter. Teaching multiple mappings (where one phoneme represents more than one grapheme or one grapheme represents more than one phoneme), as recommended by the NLS and certain phonics programmes, is of little value as the majority occur rarely and potentially confuse children as there is no logical basis for selecting one representation rather than another.

It is assumed that phonic skills are best taught in conjunction with reading schemes rather than real books. However, their limitations, particularly for low-achieving pupils, have been well documented. These children rarely become 'free readers' and so quickly lose interest and motivation. Furthermore, recent research has demonstrated that the structure of real books and reading schemes is similar and the claimed advantages of reading schemes are questionable (Solity and Vousden, 2006). Rose recognizes the potential value of real books when noting that they can fulfil 'much the same function' as decodable books (DfES, 2006: para. 84).

There are few issues raised by the Rose Review which were not also covered in the Bullock Report (DES, 1975). It is staggering that so little progress appears to have been made in over 30 years. Will the Review be seen to signal another swing in the pendulum back towards teaching phonics, or represent a substantial and enduring shift in practice? Potentially, the status of the Review will be judged on whether the outcomes for the lowest 25 per cent change in the future.

Recent research (Shapiro and Solity, 2006; Solity and Shapiro, 2006) suggests that two critical changes need to occur in practice. The first is that, contrary to conventional wisdom, lower-achieving pupils are best taught through a combination of real books and a small, optimal number of core phonic and sight vocabulary skills. Second, they should be taught through differentiated, whole class teaching, which meets a diverse range of needs.

The Review is informed by research. It would be a fitting tribute and legacy if outstanding questions and concerns were also examined through appropriate mainstream, classroom-based experimental investigations, delivered by teachers rather than researchers, so that future decisions about what to teach are research, rather than rhetoric, based.

Synthetic Arguments

Michael Rosen

The announcement that the government is going to force schools to teach children to read using synthetic phonics is a sledge-hammering political intervention into a matter that needs flexibility, subtlety and humanity. My own view is that the decision can be explained quite simply according to the David Blunkett formula of policy-making: if the Right says it's good, we'll go for it too.

The conclusions drawn from the research that claims to prove the effectiveness of synthetic phonics (Johnston and Watson, 2005) cannot be sustained. They commit the cardinal sin of all conclusions from experiments: they fail to compare like with like. That is to say, the conditions under which the children were taught using synthetic phonics were not held constant and identical with the conditions of children learning how to read by other methods. As Susan Ellis (University of Strathclyde) has shown, there is a lot of variability between the schools in question, many of which were assisted and resourced (very well) by a number of other programmes running simultaneously and in support of the synthetic phonics programme (Ellis, 2005). Before drawing conclusions from a piece of research, the question that has to be asked is: Can it be replicated? And we have a definitive answer: We don't know. In other words, government policy has been made on the evidence of an experiment from which certain conclusions cannot be made and the experiment has not been through trials. If it was a drug that was about to be unleashed on children with this kind of research, there would be an injunction to stop it being used.

Meanwhile, there's one thing we know for certain about learning how to read: we do not know exactly how it is that each and every single child does it. What's more, even when we think we know, it's quite possible that we don't. I'll explain that: it is simply not possible to summate every single relevant language experience that a child has which may lead that child to be able to read. For example, crucial breakthroughs in cracking the problem might be achieved by a child reading crisp packets, playing on her older sibling's computer, reading advertisements, learning stories off by heart and finding them in books, writing thank you letters for birthday presents and so on.

The excitement about phonics can be traced to its apparent simplicity. Many people imagine that our spelling is an organized system for indicating sounds and, vice versa, that the sounds we make with our mouths are represented systematically by letters. Neither of these two propositions is true. Using the famous c-a-t case: the letter 'c' can make a variety of sounds and vice versa, the hard 'c' sound can be spelled in at least two other ways ('k' and 'ck'); the 'a' sound in the middle of 'cat' is, yes, always made with 'a' but the letter itself is used to make a variety of sounds; the 't' at the end of 'cat' is nearly always pronounced differently when it begins a word, in some words it's silent ('castle'), while the sound at the end of 'cat' is often made by, for example, the '-ed' ending on some verbs.

The way all phonic systems work is by pretending that the letters (or combinations of letters) regularly make one sound. Then, based on that simplified system, you present the child with those words that conform. If this is the dominant method being used (which is what the government is demanding), then in a stroke you deprive children of two things:

- a set of strategies with which to manage the vast amount of reading that doesn't fit the simplified system; and
- a good deal of time spent proving that reading is a worthwhile and interesting thing to do.

Virtually every initiative taken by this government has made classrooms places that are less and less likely to spend time providing this. Children are human beings, with drives, culture, habits and feelings. Books deal with these human characteristics. Learning how to say a set of words that fit the phonics bill pays no attention to them. Those children who have already been convinced that reading a whole book will be a great thing to do (probably by their parents reading to them) will have little or no problem making the leap from phonics to real books and staying with them. For the millions of others who aren't convinced that reading is interesting or cool, no matter how good they are with their phonics, it's not clear why or how they will want to stick with it.

Rose-tinted Spectacles: Synthetic Phonics, Research Evidence and the Teaching of Reading

Dominic Wyse

After the media attention given to the interim Rose report, the release of the final report was something of a quiet affair. But it shouldn't have been. The Rose Review represents one of the most controversial documents on the teaching of reading in England ever to be released. For example, it is the first official publication to recommend the real book approach!

> There is no doubt, too, that the simple text in some recognized favourite children's books can fulfil much the same function as that of decodable books. Thus it may be possible to use these texts in parallel, *or in place of them*. (DfES, 2006: 27, my italics)

Well, if not whole-hearted advocacy of the real book approach, it does offer minimal recognition of the significance of children's literature, at least for supporting decoding.

This, of course, isn't the most controversial aspect at all; it is the lack of attention paid to the wealth of research evidence on the teaching of reading. Rose concluded that:

> Having considered a wide range of evidence, the review has concluded that the case for systematic phonic work is overwhelming and much strengthened by a synthetic approach. (DfES, 2006: 20)

The research evidence is quite clear on the question of whether synthetic phonics is better than other phonics approaches. The Department for Education and Skills-funded research review, which was completed during the time of the Rose enquiry and which included one of the advisers to the Rose enquiry, concluded that 'There is currently no strong RCT evidence that any one form of systematic phonics is more effective than any other' (Torgerson et al., 2006: 49). This was in line with the influential American National Reading Panel, which said that 'specific systematic phonics programs are all significantly more effective than non-phonics programs; however, they do not appear to differ significantly from each other in their effectiveness' (National Reading Panel, 93).

As I reported in Wyse (2000), the research does show evidence that children's word reading can be enhanced by systematic phonics teaching contextualized within a rich literate environment particularly for children aged between five and seven. Twenty out of the 43 studies covered by the NRP and the Torgerson review were carried out with children aged six to seven. Only nine studies were carried out with 5 to 6-year-olds. No studies were carried out with 4-year-olds or younger. It is also important to note that these phonics instruction studies showed gains for whole-language philosophies such as oral reading of stories and discussion; language-based reading activities; language development training; a focus on comprehension; and embedded (or contextualized) teaching of phonics. The idea that children younger than five will benefit from the kind of *synthetic* phonics programme advocated by some contributors to the Rose Review is not supported by research evidence, and is one of its most worrying recommendations.

It is extraordinary that a report on a subject of such importance fails to exploit fully the research evidence because of alleged 'uncertainties'. Instead, claims are made on the basis of inspection evidence and the ambiguous notion of 'leading-edge practice'. Rose claims that:

> Despite the content of phonic work being a statutory component of the National Curriculum over that time [1989 to 1998], HMI reports show that it was often a neglected or weak feature of the teaching. (DfES, 2006: 12)

Even this use of inspection evidence is not sufficiently balanced. In 1990, the HMI report (Ofsted, 1995) observed that in the teaching of reading in England 'phonic skills were taught almost universally and usually to beneficial effect' (1995: 2) and that 'Successful teachers of reading and the majority of schools used a mix of methods each reinforcing the other as the children's reading developed' (1995: 15). During 1993–94, inspection evidence found that 'In most schools pupils acquire satisfactory phonics skills and a range of strategies for understanding printed texts' (1995: 6). This picture accorded with research which found regular and judicial use of phonics teaching as part of a balanced approach to be the norm (Cato et al., 1992).

The main piece of research used by the Rose Review is the Clackmannanshire study (Johnston and Watson, 2005). Resigned to the fact that the study 'received some criticism by researchers', its use is defended by a focus on the classroom practice that was featured. In that case, why use this study and not one of the hundreds of other studies about reading teaching? Or, why not look at other kinds of reading pedagogy that have been successful, including whole-language teaching?

The Rose Review remit would have been more useful if it had required an examination of the NLS as a whole, including addressing the question of whether it should be replaced with something better. As far as phonics is concerned, there is an urgent need for another round of the 'reading wars' to ensure that any revisions to the NLS represent a truly evidence-informed picture. The danger of a renewed emphasis on synthetic phonics is that other equally important practices may not receive the full attention that they deserve.

Poor Mr Rose!

David Wray

You have to feel a bit sorry for Jim Rose. He has been involved in primary education at the very highest level for many years, as a senior HMI he has guided policy and practice, and as a member of the 'Three Wise Men' he had an enormous impact upon the nature of primary teaching in this country. Yet, as his career draws to its close, what is it that he will be most remembered for by primary teachers? I fear it will be as the man who said that young children were not allowed to read books until they had mastered their 44 phonemes. 'Phonics first and fast' may well be his lasting epitaph!

All of which is a bit unfair really. Especially as that is not quite what he actually says in his final report. On page 3, for example, Mr Rose states, 'the introduction of phonic work should always be a matter for principled, professional judgement based on structured observations and assessments of children's capabilities' (DfES, 2006). There is probably not a single teacher, commentator or parent who would disagree with this claim. Yet the result of this report will be to supplant such 'principled, professional judgement' with the requirements of 'the programme' of teaching phonics. Mr Rose himself lays great stress on 'fidelity to the programme', which seems to mean that a teaching programme should be followed to its bitter end even if it is manifestly not working for individuals or groups of children.

Again, on page 16, Mr Rose claims that 'It is widely agreed that phonic work is an essential part, but not the whole picture, of what it takes to become a fluent reader and skilled writer, well capable of comprehending and composing text' (DfES, 2006). It is a shame, then, that his report is being claimed as thorough vindication of the position of those extremists who claim that phonics work is the whole picture for beginning readers. One such person, the writer of a commercial teaching programme focused on phonics, even claims that her programme 'is intended to replace the National Literacy Strategy for those children who are in the early stages of learning to read (at or below NC level 2b)' (Miskin, 2004: 4). The children encompassed by this definition include the majority of children at key stage 1. So 'the whole picture' for these children will therefore be phonics work, not the more rounded and balanced programme which the NLS currently suggests, and which Mr Rose's claim seems to support.

So, what is going on here? The cynical interpretation is that, however balanced and 'wise' a report Jim Rose has written, the damage has already been done. Government ministers, and Rose himself, try to dress the report's recommendations as based on a consensus derived from research. This is actually nonsense (although establishing that would take much more space than I currently have available). What has actually happened is that pressure groups with axes to grind (and, usually, teaching programmes to sell) have caught the ear of politicians and the Rose Review was never going to be a balanced interpretation of the evidence. So, whatever the 'wise' statements that Mr Rose makes, his report will be remembered for the imposition on our children of a uni-dimensional approach to the teaching of a multi-dimensional process. And when this fails, as it inevitably will, Mr Rose will bear a large share of the blame.

Poor Mr Rose!

Chapter 11

Using this Book for Staff Development

Sue Ellis and Maureen Lewis

Effective staff development is always going to be complicated. Education is a complex matter and literacy education particularly so. An effective reading curriculum impacts widely on children's experience of, and success at, school. It is important that schools and teachers get the reading curriculum right and that staff development effects real change in classrooms and in teaching.

The research on rolling-out school reforms shows that getting the reading curriculum right in schools is not a simple matter of choosing a successful teaching programme, distributing the resources and asking teachers to get on with it. Even with vigilant monitoring, programmes and resources that are highly successful in one context may not be successful in others. This is not because they are good or bad per se, but because the way that a programme is introduced, managed and used within the school is as crucial to its success as the content and design of the programme itself (Coburn, 2003).

Achieving successful change

Various factors influence the success of a new programme. Blackmore argues that when standardized programmes are imposed in ways that ignore the local context, it creates a 'culture of compliance' in which the only thing teachers want to know about a new initiative is 'how to do it as painlessly as possible' (1998: 472). The absence of genuine intellectual engagement means that staff understanding of the content and design is often superficial and lacks the grounding essential for effective and responsive teaching. Moreover, superficially committed teachers are slower to identify and solve problems as they arise. This further impacts on the programme's success.

When changes to literacy policy are initiated by central government and monitored by external inspections, it would be easy to see schools and teachers as passive victims of circumstance. But the context for implementation is created by the practical things that real people do (Datnow et al., 2002). Teachers, classroom assistants, literacy co-ordinators, head teachers and school governors create and control the experiences, structures and culture within their school. They create the local context of implementation and thus determine the impact any new phonics programme or resource will have.

Ownership and empowerment

A key factor in successful change is the extent to which school staff understand and buy-in to the new ideas. Staff buy-in will increase if a new phonics initiative is clearly located within the school's wider literacy curriculum and if they can see how it contributes to the long-term strategic plan to raise attainment and benefit the children (Ofsted, 2004).

Success is also more likely when teachers feel empowered, and central to this is respect for the knowledge and experience they bring. 'Uniform change' and 'effective change' may not be the same thing. Co-ordinators and head teachers who see their role as policemen protecting the fidelity of a bought-in phonics programme are likely to be less successful than those who see their role as hands-on facilitators whose aim is to help staff integrate the programme into their teaching and work out how to use it most effectively to meet the needs of the children. Reform models with such flexibility are also more sustainable.

Effective facilitators will introduce and implement staff development on phonics in ways that deepen professional understandings and support changes in pedagogy. At the same time, they will encourage teachers to mould the initiative to ensure that it fits well with the school's wider literacy strategy and with pupils' learning.

Good leaders are able to keep people going, remind them of their successes and keep them focused. Although they have a vision of how they would like things to be, they are not totally blinded by it; they listen to what others say. When school reforms fail, the head teacher is often seen as supporting the reform from a distance rather than directly leading it (Datnow et al., 2002). In highly effective schools, head teachers are seen as the instructional leaders, with a clear understanding of how reading is taught, assessed and monitored (Ofsted, 2004).

The first point when considering the school's policy and practice on phonics teaching, is for all staff, including the senior management team, to think about the issue from different angles:

- *The children's learning*: Do the children find the content of the phonics programme intellectually interesting, and do they have sufficient opportunities to practise and apply their new knowledge and skills?
- *The children's achievements*: Does the existing phonics programme achieve good results for the children, in line with, or better than, other schools with similar intakes?
- *The wider literacy curriculum*: New initiatives often have a 'ripple effect' on other teaching and may distort the wider aims of the curriculum. It is important to ensure a balanced, coherent experience for children. The bottom line is that the phonics programme should contribute to a successful, engaging and emotionally satisfying literacy curriculum, not become an end in itself.
- *The staff's capacity to deliver*: Different beliefs about literacy, different understandings of phonics and different experiences of teaching the literacy curriculum all affect how a new initiative will be interpreted and implemented. Staff may need to consider their own content knowledge as well as the content and sequence, pace and variety of their phonics teaching and how they nudge and support children to apply and use their phonic knowledge in new situations.

Encouraging teachers and classroom assistants to describe what they do, how they do it and the next steps they might take develops content knowledge and ensures ownership of the curriculum. Analytical discussion of specific children and of how to move their learning forward, deepens content knowledge and broadens pedagogical understanding. Working from specific examples enables educators to link theory and practice within a particular context. Research shows that whole staff identification of issues, followed by agreed action to address the issues and sharing the outcomes, is a powerful form of professional development (EPPI, 2003). Whole staff discussion is a vital first step in this process.

Staff development

Deepening knowledge and skills is central to any professional development. Teachers obviously need subject knowledge about phonics and a strong repertoire of teaching activities to ensure that children develop and use their phonic knowledge. They also need to be 'noticing teachers', who are sufficiently flexible and analytical to spot children who are not being challenged or who are struggling, and be confident enough to do something about them.

Ofsted (2002) notes that schools are beginning to adopt a wider and more comprehensive view of professional development. The most effective developments are likely to be embedded in the curriculum and in teachers' concerns. They allow 'cooking time' for new ideas, space for teachers to experiment and practise, and they allow opportunities to analyse children's learning with others.

There does, however, need to be a clear focus and drive. Boyle et al. (2005) note that the most common staff development activities in England were observation of colleagues and sharing practice, but 'coaching' and 'research inquiry' were reported as having most impact. Study groups involving regular, sustained and collaborative work on topics chosen by the group as well as coaching or mentoring arrangements, where teachers work with an equally or more experienced colleague, have both proved successful.

How this book can help

If teachers are to feel empowered rather than undermined by change in the literacy curriculum, they need some input into the development agenda. But discussion must be informed by an up-to-date knowledge of research and best practice if it is not to become a cosy confirmation of prior beliefs. Chapters of this book can be used as study guides to prompt and guide the group discussions that will help the whole school progress towards confident and coherent change.

One strategy is for groups of staff to design their own study and discussion sequence, perhaps around the issues detailed below.

Locate phonics within the wider literacy curriculum

For years, the subject of phonics has polarized professional debate. Teachers are likely to have different and compelling opinions about how much phonics should be taught, when, and how quickly, as well as different understandings of successful teaching activities for phonics and of how phonic knowledge can be useful to developing readers and writers.

These professional differences need to be acknowledged in a way that locates them within a complex conversation about teaching reading rather than as simplistic polarized debating positions. Some teachers may fear that a renewed focus on phonics will lead to an over-emphasis on the mechanics of reading and a lack of attention to aspects such as reading engagement and comprehension. Others may be keen to explore whether a stronger and more structured emphasis on phonics could supplement the current literacy programme and further empower children as readers and writers. A third group may welcome a strong phonics programme because it appears to offer a more linear, prescribed and 'certain' curriculum. They may interpret a focus on phonics as giving them 'permission' to omit aspects that they currently find difficult and complex.

Discussion of Chapters 1 and 2 can help to raise these issues in a non-confrontational way. As they discuss which ideas are new to them, which they agree with and which they do not, staff will be articulating:

- their own values, beliefs and assumptions about reading and learning to read;
- what they believe to be important and effective about their own practice; and
- their observations of children and of possible benefits that could result from a review of phonics teaching in the school.

It goes without saying that discussion needs to be collegiate and reflective, rather than argumentative and confrontational. Explicit acknowledgement that the ultimate aim of the reading curriculum is to help children make sense of and respond to text may be important, along with detailed discussions of how any changes in teaching phonics might contribute to this.

Find an authentic starting point: target staff knowledge and skills

Successful development initiatives either have good buy-in from staff at the start or they establish it quickly. It is important that teachers quickly identify specific benefits for their own knowledge and understanding and for the curriculum, the children and the school.

Studies show that there is considerable variability in how phonics programmes are delivered. This means that teachers will undoubtedly realize different benefits from a review of phonics teaching. In England, Ofsted (2004) reports that the best phonics teaching is systematic and that teaching sessions are frequent, short and brisk. Effective teachers are well-informed, build on what pupils already know and develop their confidence. Ineffective phonics teaching is often too slow and not systematic. Low teacher expectations and poor teacher content knowledge lead to confused and boring lessons.

Two chapters will raise these issues for discussion. Chapter 4, in which three teachers present different accounts of effective phonics teaching, will help teachers to identify and discuss aspects of their own practice and can provide a springboard for raising issues about coherence and change.

Staff may use the information in Chapter 3 to deepen their own content knowledge. They will need time to discuss the content, identify implications for their own practice, experiment with changes and monitor the effects. The issues arising from this may provide a good basis for peer coaching sessions. In terms of policy, the chapter may deepen understanding of:

- the sequence of sounds covered;
- how systematically sounds are covered;
- how quickly sounds are covered;
- the pace of teaching and the range of teaching activities used; and
- how and when the children use phonics in reading and spelling.

Consider the learners

Any focus on teaching needs to be balanced by a consideration of learning. Good teachers notice when children appear not to understand phonics, but often don't know what to do about this. Chapter 6 explains the articulatory basis of speech and how to identify children who may need additional help or a different kind of help with phonic work.

Make links to writing and spelling and understand the limitations of phonics

Successful readers and writers have a high level of self-efficacy; they believe in their abilities and will 'have a go' at applying their knowledge and skills in new contexts. They are not deterred by the thought of making mistakes and tend to see problems as things to resolve only when and if they arise. Young children's self-efficacy is often tightly localized to particular tasks. Teachers need to promote self-efficacy and confidence by encouraging children to use their phonic knowledge for both reading and writing. When this happens, the children use their phonic knowledge more frequently and the additional practice feeds an upward spiral of attainment in which the practice consolidates the learning, makes skills more automatic and further develops confidence. Chapter 7 provides the content knowledge and background to help teachers do this effectively in relation to spelling. Chapter 8 explains the limitations of this within a language that is not always phonically regular in a way that will equip teachers to make their teaching informed and flexible.

Consider the child beyond school

Families are important influences on how children progress in school. Information needs to flow in two directions. Schools need to know about the rhymes, songs, stories, books (both fiction and non-fiction) and multi-modal texts that children enjoy at home, and actively ensure that the school curriculum acknowledges and builds on this. Families are also important allies for teachers, and schools need to communicate their views about phonics as part of their literacy policy and enlist parents' help where possible. Chapter 5 will inform discussion of this.

Put policy in perspective

It is detrimental when education reforms are seen as short-term 'cures' (Datnow et al., 2002). Where effective schools work strategically and keep in mind long-term goals, ineffective ones tend to have one-off events (Ofsted, 2004). An understanding of the historical context can help teachers to appreciate how ideas have evolved and why an initiative gains credence at a particular point in time. Chapter 9 places phonics teaching within an historical context and reminds everyone of the importance of keeping a sense of perspective and balance within the literacy curriculum. Finally, Chapter 10 shows the breadth of views that still exist and are likely to exist within any school community.

Glossary

Affricates	The sounds made in speech when the air-stream is stopped as for a plosive but released as for a fricative sound. English affricates are 'ch' and 'j'.
Assimilation	Describes how the articulation of phonemes is influenced by, and accommodates to, the articulation of the surrounding sounds during rapid, connected speech.
Alphabetic code/ alphabetic principle	A system used for writing where graphemes formed from letters represent sounds.
Analytic phonics	A whole-to-part teaching approach in which children do not learn each phoneme in isolation, but might discuss and analyse a number of words containing the sound and are helped to see letter patterns and draw analogies with other words. In writing a new word, analytic phonics programmes would encourage the child to think of similar-sounding words they can write and use this knowledge to work out how to write the new word.
Big book	A larger version of a children's book, used for sharing and discussing the text with the whole class.
Blend/blending	Often known as 'phonemic blending'. Merging individual phonemes together to pronounce a word, for example, 'c-a-t' blended together makes 'cat'. To read an unknown word the child must recognize each grapheme, not each letter, for example, 'th-a-t', not 't-h-a-t'.

Closed class	A category of words or parts of speech that rarely acquires new members, for example, pronouns such as 'he', 'she'; conjunctions such as 'and', 'that', or determiners such as 'the', 'an'. It contrasts with 'open class' word categories such as nouns and verbs, to which new words are quite commonly added.
Consonant clusters	Also known as adjacent or consecutive consonants. Two (or three) letters making two (or three) sounds. For example, the first two letters of 'brake' and the first three letters of 'string' are consonant clusters. Consonant clusters should not be confused with digraphs.
Concepts about print/ conventions of print	The understandings about the rules or accepted practices that govern readers' and writers' use of print. For example: understanding that English texts are read left to right, top to bottom, left page before right, that words consist of letters and that spaces indicate the boundaries between words and so on.
Consonant	The sounds made when breath from the lungs is stopped or occluded before it emerges from the mouth. They can be voiced or voiceless.
Cursive font/writing	A style of handwriting where letters are joined to produce a continuous joined script.
CVC/CCVC words	Abbreviations for consonant and vowel, used to show the consonant/vowel structure of words, for example, dog is a CVC word; stop is a CCVC word and stamp is a CCVCC word.
Decodable books	Books written with a vocabulary that is restricted to words made up of the phoneme–letter correspondences that have been taught.
Decoding	Usually understood to mean reading an unknown word by sounding out and blending the phonemes represented by the letters. A reader can decode a word without knowing what it means. However, in psychology 'decoding' means accessing the print on the page. This can include both reading words automatically as well as by blending sounds.

Deep orthography (opaque orthography)	A writing system that does not have consistent or one-to-one correspondence between the phonemes and morphemes of the language and the graphemes. English is an example of a deep orthography.
Digraph/vowel digraph/split digraph	A two-lettered grapheme. Two letters making one sorund, for example, consonant digraphs 'th' and 'ch'; vowel digraphs 'oo', 'ai', 'ow'. A split digraph is where the two letters of the digraph are separated by a consonant, for example, 'a-e' in 'take' or 'o-e' in 'bone'.
Diphthong	A vowel in which there is a perceptible change in quality during the syllable (as in 'fear', 'coin').
Environmental print	Words and symbols seen in the environment and used in everyday life, such as product labels, logos and traffic signs.
Fricatives	The sounds made where two parts of the mouth or throat come so close together that we hear the turbulence in the air stream. (English fricatives are: 'f' as in 'fish'; 'v' as in 'verve'; 's' as in 'soap'; 'z' as in 'zoo'; 'sh' as in 'shy'; 'zh' as in the middle of 'treasure'; 'th' as in 'this' and 'their'. Scottish English has two more: 'wh' as in 'which' and 'ch' as in 'loch', and Welsh adds 'll' sound illustrated by the first sound in the word 'Llanelli'.
Glides (liquid sounds)	Sounds made by air passing through the mouth more freely than for stops or fricatives, but less freely than for vowels. English glide sounds are 'l', 'r', 'w', 'y'.
Grapheme	A letter or group of letters that are the written representation of a phoneme, for example, 'a', 't', 'ch', 'kn' or 'ough' (as in though).
Graphological awareness	The developing awareness of print. How grapheme can be used to represent and manipulate meaning.
Guided reading	With beginning readers, the teacher provides support for a small group reading a book that is at an instructional level of difficulty, helping them to use

reading cues and strategies independently. In shared/supported reading, the teacher may be reading with the whole class and the book may be at a level beyond that which the children could read independently.

Letter–sound correspondence/ phoneme–grapheme correspondence/ grapheme–phoneme correspondences (GPC)

These terms all refer to the relationship between sounds and the letters that represent those sounds.

Logographic

A system where one written symbol, or logo, represents a whole word. For example, the International Red Cross sign or Chinese script.

Long-term memory

Stores information and knowledge about the world over a long period of time, creating schema which influence how we attend to future information.

High-frequency words

About 100 words that make up roughly half of all the words occurring in most non-technical texts. Because these words occur so frequently in text, teachers aim to ensure that children can recognize them easily when reading and read them rapidly 'on sight'.

Mnemonic

A sentence or phrase that aids memory/recall. Mnemonics can be used as an aid to remember how to spell a word (for example, 'because' – **b**ig **e**lephants **c**annot **a**lways **u**se **s**mall **e**xits) or to recall a letter shape (for example, a snake for the letter 's').

Morpheme

The smallest unit of meaning in a language. For example, the word 'talk' is one morpheme, but 'talked' is two morphemes; 'talk' plus the past tense marker 'ed'.

Morphological

Based on the meaning of stem words and their added morphemes.

Name game

A game common in New Zealand. Children orally identify the first sound in their name by saying 'My name is . . . It begins with . . .'.

National Literacy Strategy (NLS)	The NLS is a non-statutory, government-funded initiative for improving children's achievements in literacy in England. It consists of a framework of teaching objectives, professional development materials for teachers and classroom materials, promoted via a national network of literacy consultants.
Onset and rime	The onset of a syllable is the consonant or consonant cluster at the beginning of the syllable and before the vowel. The rime is the vowel and any consonants that follow. Syllables beginning with a vowel (for example, 'egg') have no onset.
Orthography	The complete writing system for the language.
Phonemes	Single identifiable sounds of language, for example, the letters 'th' represent just one sound, but 'sp' represents two, /s/ and /p/. Phonemes make the contrasts between words so that changing the phoneme changes the meaning, for example, 'cat', 'that', 'sat'.
Phonemic awareness	The ability to recognize and manipulate the individual sounds in a word.
Phonemic blending – (see Blend/blending)	Combining individual phonemes to form a word or syllable.
Phonemic segmentation	The skill required to segment words into individual phonemes.
Phonics teaching/instruction	Teaching that is focused on the relationships between letters and sounds.
Phonetics	A science studying the characteristics of, and providing methods for, the description, classification and transcription of human sound-making, particularly speech sounds.
Phonographic	A system where written letters represent speech sounds.
Phonological access	How quickly phonological information can be retrieved. It is measured by rapid naming tasks.

Phonological analysis	The ability to identify or isolate phonemes from words.
Phonological awareness	The conscious awareness of, and ability to manipulate, phonology. It requires sensitivity to, or explicit awareness of, the phonological structure of the words in language.
Phonological knowledge	Knowledge of the sounds and sound patterns of a language.
Phonological memory	The brief retention in working memory of non-meaningful sequences of letters, digits or spoken non-words.
Phonological processing	A general term referring to the processes used to identify, contrast, manipulate, produce and remember speech sounds.
Phonological synthesis	The ability to blend phonemes presented separately into whole words.
Phonology	The study of the sound system of language, or the sound system itself.
Plosive	The sound made when the air from the lungs is completely stopped for a short time in the mouth, then released. Also called a 'stop'. English plosives are 'p', 'b', 't', 'd', 'k', 'g'.
Quadragraph	Four letters that make one sound, for example, 'ough' as in 'ought'.
Reading cues	The graphophonic, syntactic and semantic clues that prompt a reader to decode and make sense of text.
Reading Recovery	A one-to-one teaching intervention designed by New Zealander Dame Marie Clay to identify, analyse, teach and monitor the progress of children who, one year after starting school, need to 'catch-up' with their peers.
Rhyming strings	A number of words that all rhyme with each other.

Rime	The part of a syllable that contains the vowel and any consonant or consonant cluster that might come after the first vowel. The rime in the word 'tea' has no consonants. The rime in the word 'teach' is 'each'.
Segmenting	Hearing and breaking a word up into its individual phonemes, for example, 'th-a-t', or into syllables, for example, 'rep-re-sent'.
Semantic	Pertaining to meaning.
Shallow orthography	See Transparent orthography.
Supported reading	See Guided reading.
Syntax/syntactic	The rules, or grammar, that govern sentence structure.
Synthetic phonics	Comes from the word 'sythesize' – bring together. In synthetic phonics the phonemes (sounds) associated with particular graphemes (letters) are each isolated, pronounced and blended together (synthesized) to read and write the word. For example, when reading an unknown single-syllable word such as 'dog', the child would sound out its three phonemes and then blend them together. In writing, the child would segment the word into its individual phonemes and say and write them. In synthetic phonics programmes, children are systematically taught phoneme–grapheme correspondences. They learn the sounds represented by letters and letter combinations, blend these sounds to pronounce words, and finally identify which phonic generalizations apply.
THRASS	A picture-based programme to Teach Handwriting, Reading And Spelling Skills.
Transparent (shallow) orthography	A writing system in which there is a consistent correspondence between the phonemes of the language and the graphemes. Finnish is an example of a language with a transparent orthography.
Trigraph	Three letters making one sound (phoneme), for example, 'dge' in 'bridge' or 'tch' in 'itch'. A three-letter grapheme.

Voiced   When air from the lungs is given a 'buzz' from the vocal cords vibrating together. In English, the sounds 'd' and 'b' are voiced and compare to their unvoiced counterparts 't' and 'p'.

Voiceless   When air passes through the larynx without the vocal cords vibrating.

Vowel   The sound made when breath from the lungs is given a buzz from the vocal cords vibrating together but not stopped or occluded in other ways. English words contain at least one vowel. In the alphabet a, e, i, o, u (y) are known as vowels and they are used in all the graphemes that form vowel digraphs and trigraphs. The letters 'w', 'y' and 'r' are also used, for example, 'ow', 'ay' and 'ar'.

Vowel owl   A permanent, working wall display. Pictures of big owls sit on a tree, each with a vowel on its breast. The teacher or a child chooses a vowel owl for the day and children look for words that have that particular vowel in them. At first they point the vowel out, but as the year progresses, they write the word and circle the vowel before pinning it to the tree.

Working memory The temporary storage of information being processed.

References

Adams, M.J. (1990) *Beginning to Read: Thinking and Learning About Print*. Cambridge, MA: MIT Press.

Adams, M.J., Foorman, B., Lundberg, I. and Beeler, T. (1998) *Phonemic Awareness in Young Children*. Baltimore, MD: Paul H. Brookes.

Augur, J. and Briggs, S. (1992) *Hickey Multi-Sensory Language Course*. London: Whurr.

Baker, L., Mackler, K., Sonnenschein, S. and Serpell, R. (2001) 'Parent interactions with their first-grade children during storybook reading and relations with subsequent home reading activity and reading achievement', *Journal of School Psychology*, 39: 415–38.

Baker, L., Scher, D. and Mackler, K. (1997) 'Home and family influences on motivations for readings', *Educational Psychologist*, 32: 69–82.

Bayley, R. and Broadbent, L. (2005) *Flying Start with Literacy: Activities for Parents and Children*. Stafford: Network Educational Press.

Bell, D. (2005) 'A Good Read'. Speech to Mark World Book Day, 2 March.

Bielby, N. (1994) *Making Sense of Reading: The New Phonics and Its Practical Implications*. Warwickshire: Scholastic.

Bissex, G. (1980) *GNYS AT WRK: A Child Learns to Write and Read*. Cambridge, MA: Harvard University Press.

Blackmore, J. (1998) 'The politics of gender and educational change', in A. Hargreaves, A. Lieberman, M. Fullan and D. Hopkins (eds), *International Handbook of Educational Change*. Norwell, MA: Kluwer Academic. pp. 460–81.

Blakemore, S.J. and Frith, U. (2005) *The Learning Brain: Lessons for Education*. Oxford: Blackwell.

Bowey, J.A. (2002) 'Reflections on onset–rime and phoneme sensitivity as predictors of beginning word reading', *Journal of Experimental Child Psychology*, 82: 29–40.

Bowey, J.A. (2005) 'Predicting individual differences in learning to read', in M.J. Snowling and C. Hulme (eds), *The Science of Reading: A Handbook*. Oxford: Blackwell. pp. 155–72.

Boyle, B., Lamprianou, I. and Boyle, T. (2005) 'A longitudinal study of teacher change: What makes professional development effective? Report of the second year of the study', *Journal of School Effectiveness and School Improvement*, 16 (1): 1–27.

Bragg, M. (2004) *The Adventure of English*. London: Sceptre.

Bryant, P. (2002) 'Children's thoughts about reading and spelling', *Scientific Studies of Reading*, 6 (2): 199–216.

Bryant, P. and Bradley, L. (1980) 'Why children sometimes write words which they do not read', in U. Frith (ed.), *Cognitive Processes in Spelling*. London: Academic Press. pp. 352–73.

Bryant, P. and Bradley, L. (1985) *Children's Reading Problems*. Oxford: Blackwell.

Bryant, P.E., Nunes, T. and Bindman, M. (1997) 'Children's understanding of the connection between grammar and spelling', in B. Blachman (ed.), *Linguistic Underpinnings of Reading*. Hillsdale, NJ: Erlbaum. pp. 219–40.

Bryant, P.E., Nunes, T. and Snaith, R. (2000) 'Children learn an untaught rule of spelling', *Nature*, 403 (6766): 157.

Bryson, B. (1970) *Mother Tongue: The English Language*. Harmondsworth: Penguin.

Bus, A.G. and van Ijzendoorn, M.H. (1999) 'Phonological awareness and early reading: A meta-analysis of experimental training studies', *Journal of Educational Psychology*, 91: 403–14.

Bussis, A., Chittenden, E., Amarel, A. and Klausner, E. (1985) *Inquiry into Meaning: An Investigation into Learning to Read*. Hillsdale, NJ: Erlbaum.

Byrne, B. (1998) *The Foundation of Literacy: The Child's Acquisition of the Alphabetic Principle*. Hove: Psychology Press.

Byrne, B. (2005) 'Theories of learning to read', in M.J. Snowling and C. Hulme (eds), *The Science of Reading: A Handbook*. Oxford: Blackwell. pp. 104–19.

Carney, E. (1994) *A Survey of English Spelling*. London: Routledge.

Carnine, D.W., Silbert, J. and Kameenui, E.J. (1997) *Direct Instruction Reading*. Englewood Cliffs, NJ: Prentice Hall.

Carrington, V. amd Luke, A. (2003) 'Reading, homes and families: From postmodern to modern?', in A. van Kleeck, S.A. Stahl, and E.B. Bauer (eds), *On Reading to Children: Parents and Teachers*. Mahwah, NJ: Erlbaum.

Carroll, J.B., Davies, P. and Richman, B. (1971) *The American Heritage Word Frequency Book*. New York: Houghton Mifflin.

Castles, A. and Coltheart, M. (2004) 'Is there a causal link from phonological awareness to success in learning to read?', *Cognition*, 91: 77–111.

Cataldo, S. and Ellis, N. (1988) 'Interactions in the development of spelling, reading and phonological skills', *Journal of Research in Reading*, 11 (2): 86–109.

Cato, V., Fernandes, C., Gorman, T., Kispal, A. and White, J. (1992) *The Teaching of Initial Literacy: How do Teachers Do It?* Slough: National Foundation for Educational Research.

Chall, J.S. (1967) *Learning to Read: The Great Debate*. New York: McGraw Hill.

Chew, J. (1997) 'Traditional phonics: What it is and what it is not', *Journal of Research in Reading*, 20 (3): 171–83.

Chomsky, C. (1979) 'Approaching reading through invented spelling', in L.B. Resnick and P.A. Weaver (eds), *Theory and Practice of Early Reading*. Hillsdale, NJ: Erlbaum.

Churchill, W.S. (1930) *My Early Life*. London: Thomas Butterworth.

Clay, M. (1993) *Reading Recovery: A Guidebook for Teachers*. Auckland: Heinemann Education.

Coburn, C. (2003) 'Rethinking scale: Moving beyond numbers to deep and lasting change', *Educational Researcher*, 32 (6): 3–12.

Congdon, P.J. (1974) *Phonics Skills and their Measurement*. Oxford: Basil Blackwell.

Cook, M. (ed.) (2002) *Perspectives on the Teaching and Learning of Phonics*. Royston: United Kingdom Literacy Association.

Cossu, G., Gugliotta, M., Marshall, J.C. (1995) 'Acquisition of reading and written spelling in a transparent orthography: two non parallel processes?', *Reading and Writing*, 7: 9–22.

Cripps, C. (1991) *A Hand for Spelling: Pupil Profile*. Wisbech: LDA.

Crystal, D. (2002) *The English Language*. Harmondsworth: Penguin.

Cunningham, P.M. and Cunningham, J.W. (2002) 'What we know about how to teach phonics', in A. Farstrup and S.J. Samuels (eds), *What Research has to Say about Reading*. Delaware, NE: International Reading Association.

Datnow, A., Hubbard, L. and Mehan, H. (2002) *Extending School Reform – From One School to Many*. London: RoutledgeFalmer.

DES (Department of Education and Science) (1975) *A Language for Life*. London: HMSO.

DEST (Department of Education, Science and Training) (2004) *National Inquiry into the Teaching of Literacy*. Commonwealth of Australia.

DEST (2005) *Teaching Reading: Report and Recommendations*. Commonwealth of Australia.

Desforges, C. and Abouchaar, A. (2003) *The Impact of Parental Involvement, Parental Support and Family Education on Pupil Achievement and Adjustment: A Review of Literature*. London: HMSO.

DfEE (Department for Education and Employment) (1998a) *The National Literacy Strategy: Framework for Teaching*. London: DfEE. Available online at www.standards.dfes.gov.uk/primary/publications/literacy/nls_framework

DfEE (1998b) *Literacy Training Pack*. London: DfEE. Available online at www.standards.dfes.gov.uk/primary/publications/literacy/63585/

DfEE (1999a) *Progression in Phonics*. London: DfEE. Available online at www.standards.dfes.gov.uk/primary/publications/literacy/63305/

DfEE (1999b) *Early Literacy Support*. London: DFEE.

DfEE (1999c) *Spelling Bank KS2*. London: DfEE. Available online at www.standards.dfes.gov.uk/primary/publications/literacy/63313/

DfEE (2000) *Progression in Phonics CD-ROM*. London: DfEE. Available online at www.standards.dfes.gov.uk/primary/publications/literacy/63309/

DfES and QCA (2000) *The National Curriculum Handbook for Teachers*. London: DfES.

DfES (2001) *Developing Early Writing*. London: DfES. Available online at www.standards.dfes.gov.uk/primary/publications/literacy/63337/

DfES (2003a) *Playing with Sounds: A Supplement to Progression in Phonics*. London: DfES. Available online at www.standards.dfes.gov.uk/primary/publications/literacy/948809/

DfES (2003b) *Year 2 and Year 3 Planning Exemplification and Spelling Programme*. London: DfES. Available online at www.standards.dfes.gov.uk/primary/publications/literacy/849451/

DfES (2005a) *Independent Review of the Teaching of Early Reading: Interim Report to DfES*. London: DfES.

DfES (2005b) *National Curriculum Assessment of 11-year-olds in England*. National Statistics, First Release. London: DfES.

DfES (2006) *Independent Review of the Teaching of Early Reading* (The Rose Review). London: DfES. Available online at www.standards.dfes.gov.uk/rosereview/finalreport

DfES (in press) *Primary National Strategy Revised Framework*. London: DfES.

Diack, H. (1965) *In Spite of the Alphabet: A Study of the Teaching of Reading*. London: Chatto and Windus.

Dixon, M., Stuart, M. and Masterson, J. (2002) 'The role of phonological awareness and the development of orthographic representations', *Reading and Writing: An Interdisciplinary Journal*, 15: 295–316.

Dodd, B., Crosbie, S., McIntosh, B., Teirzel, T. and Ozanne, A. (2000) *Preschool and Primary Inventory of Phonological Awareness (PIPA)*. London: Harcourt Assessment.

Dodd, B., Holm, A., Crosbie, S. and Hua, Z. (2005) 'Children's acquisition of phonology', in B. Dodd (ed.), *Differential Diagnosis and Treatment of Children with Speech Disorder*, 2nd edn. London: Whurr. pp. 24–45.

Downing, J. (1965) *The Initial Teaching Alphabet Explained and Illustrated*. London: Cassell.

Dr Seuss (2003) *The Cat in the Hat*. London: Collins.

Education and Skills Committee (2005) *Teaching Children to Read. Eighth Report of Session 2004–05: Report, together with formal minutes, oral and written evidence.* London: The Stationery Office.

Ehri, L. (1984) 'How orthography alters spoken language competencies in children learning to reading and spell', in J. Downing and R. Valtin (eds), *Language Awareness and Learning to Read and Spell.* New York: Springer-Verlag.

Ehri, L.C. (1995) 'Phases of development in learning to read words by sight', *Journal of Research in Reading,* 18, 116–15.

Ehri, L. (2005) 'Development of sight word reading: phases and findings', in C. Hulme and M. Snowling (eds), *The Science of Reading.* Malden: Blackwell. pp. 135–54.

Ehri, L.C., Nunes, S.R., Stahl, S.A. and Willows, D.M. (2001a) 'Systematic phonics instruction helps students learn to read: Evidence from the National Reading Panel's meta-analysis', *Review of Educational Research,* 71: 393–447.

Ehri, L.C., Nunes, S.R., Willows, D.M., Schuster, B.V., Yaghoub-Zadeh, Z. and Shanahan,T. (2001b) 'Phonemic awareness instruction helps children learn to read: Evidence from the National Reading Panel's meta-analysis', *Reading Research Quarterly,* 36 (3): 250–87.

Ellis, S. (205) 'Platform: Phonics', *Times Education Supplement (Scotland),* 23 September.

EPPI (Evidence for Policy and Practice Information and Co-ordinating Centre) (2003) *The impact of collaborative CPD on classroom teaching and learning. How does collaborative Continuing Professional Development (CPD) for teachers of the 5–16 age range affect teaching and learning?* London: Social Science Research Unit, Institute of Education, University of London.

Ferreiro, E. and Teberovsky, A. (1982) *Literacy Before School.* London: Heinemann Educational.

Flesch, R. (1955) *Why Johnny Can't Read and What You Can Do about It.* New York: Harper.

Foorman, B.R., Breier, J.I. and Fletcher, J.M. (2003) 'Interventions aimed at improving reading success: An evidence-based approach', *Developmental Neuropsychology,* 24: 613–39.

Frederickson, N., Frith, U. and Reason, R. (1997) *Phonological Assessment Battery (PhAB).* London: NFER-Nelson.

Frith, U. (1985) 'Beneath the surface of developmental dyslexia', in J. Patterson, J.C. Marshall and M. Coltheart (eds), *Surface Dyslexia.* London: Erlbaum. pp. 301–30.

Frith, U., Wimmer, H. and Landerl, K. (1998) 'Differences in phonological recoding in German- and English-speaking children', *Scientific Studies of Reading,* 2 (1): 31–54.

Fuge, C. (2001) *Yip Yap Snap.* Berkeley, CA: Tricycle Press.

Gentry, R. (1982) 'An analysis of developmental spelling in GNYS AT WRK', *The Reading Teacher,* 36: 192–200.

Gontijo, P.F.D., Gontijo, I. and Shillcock, R. (2003) 'Grapheme–phoneme probabilities in British English', *Behavior Research Methods, Instruments, & Computers,* 35: 136–57.

Goodwin, P. (2005) *The Literate Classroom,* 2nd edn. London: David Fulton.

Goodwin, P. and Perkins, M. (2002) *Teaching Language and Literacy in the Early Years.* London: David Fulton.

Goswami, U. (1993) 'Toward an interactive analogy model of reading development: Decoding vowel graphemes in beginning reading', *Journal of Experimental Child Psychology,* 56: 443–75.

Goswami, U. (2002) 'Rhymes, phonemes and learning to read: Interpreting recent research', in M. Cook (ed.), *Perspectives on the Teaching and Learning of Phonics.* Royston: United Kingdom Literacy Association.

Goswami, U. (2005) 'Synthetic phonics and learning to read: A cross-language perspective', *Educational Psychology in Practice,* 21 (4): 273–82.

Gough, P.B. and Tunmer, W.E. (1986) 'Decoding, reading and reading disability', *Remedial and Special Education*, 7: 6–10.

Gregory, E., Long, S. and Volk, D. (2004) *Many Pathways to Literacy*. London: Routledge Falmer.

Guthrie, J. (2004) 'Motivating students to read: Evidence for classroom practices that increase reading motivation and achievement', in P. McCardle and V. Chhabra (eds), *The Voice of Evidence in Reading Research*. Baltimore, MD: Paul Brookes.

Hall, K. (2003a) 'Effective literacy teaching in the early years of school: A review of evidence', in N. Hall, J. Larson and J. Marsh (eds), *Handbook of Early Childhood Literacy*. London: Sage. pp. 315–26.

Hall, K. (2003b) *Listening to Stephen Read: Multiple Perspectives on Literacy*. Buckingham: Open University Press. pp. 67–101.

Hall, K. (2004) *Literacy and Schooling: Towards Renewal in Primary Education Policy*. Aldershot: Ashgate.

Hall, N. (1987) *The Emergence of Literacy*. London: Hodder and Stoughton.

Hannon, P. (2003) 'Family literacy programmes', in N. Hall, J. Larson and J. Marsh (eds), *Handbook of Early Childhood Literacy*. London: Sage.

Harrison, C. (1999) 'When scientists don't agree: The case for balanced phonics', *Reading*, 33 (2): 59–63.

Harrison, C. (2004) *Understanding Reading Development*. London: Sage.

Hatcher, P. (2000) *Sound Linkage*, 2nd edn. Chichester: Wiley.

Hatcher, P.J., Hulme, C. and Snowling, M. (2004) 'Explicit phoneme training combined with phonic reading instruction helps young children at risk of reading failure', *Journal of Child Psychology and Psychiatry*, 45: 338–58.

Hilton, M., Styles, M., and Watson, V. (eds) (1997) *Opening the Nursery Door*. London: Routledge. pp. 180–98.

Holdaway, D. (1979) *The Foundations of Literacy*. Sydney: Ashton Scholastic.

House of Commons Education and Skills Committee (2005) *Teaching Children to Read*, 8th Report of Session 2004–05. London: The Stationery Office.

Huey, E.B. (1908) *The Psychology and Pedagogy of Reading*. New York: Macmillan.

Hulme, C., Caravolas, M., Malkova, G. and Brigstocke, S. (2005) 'Phoneme isolation ability is not simply a consequence of letter-sound knowledge', *Cognition*, 97: B1–11.

Hulme, C., Hatcher, P., Nation, K., Brown, A., Adams, J. and Stuart, G. (2002) 'Phoneme awareness is a better predictor of early reading skill than onset–rime awareness', *Journal of Experimental Child Psychology*, 82: 2–28.

Hurry, J., Bryant, P., Curno, T., Nunes, T., Parker, M. and Pretzlik, U. (2005) 'Teaching and learning literacy', *Research Papers in Education*, 20 (1): 187–206.

Huxford, L., Terrell, C. and Bradley, L. (1991) 'Phonological strategies in reading and spelling', *Journal of Research in Reading*, 14 (2): 99–105.

Jansen, M. (1985) 'Language and concepts: Play or work? Seriousness or fun? Basics or creativity?', in Margaret M. Clark (ed.), *New Directions in the Study of Reading*. Lewes: Falmer.

Johnston, F.P. (2001) 'The utility of phonic generalizations: Let's take another look at Clymer's conclusions', *The Reading Teacher*, 55 (2): 132–43.

Johnston, R. and Watson, J. (2005) 'The effects of synthetic phonics teaching on reading and spelling attainment', Scottish Executive Education Department. Full report available online at www.scotland.gov.uk

Juel, C. and Minden-Cupp, C. (2001) 'Learning to read words: Linguistic units and instructional strategies', *Reading Research Quarterly*, 35 (4): 458–93.

Kemp, L. and Peters, A. (2003) *Phonological Awareness Screening Pack*. Dundee: Dundee City Council. Available online at www.ltscotland.org.uk/Images/daspectsph_tcm4–122407.pdf

Kress, G. (2000) *Early Spelling*. London: Routledge.

Kuhl, P.K. (2004) 'Early language acquisition: Cracking the speech code. *Nature Reviews/ Neuroscience*, 5: 831–43.

Leitão, S. and Fletcher, J. (2004) 'Literacy outcomes for students with speech impairment: Long term follow-up', *International Journal of Language and Communication Disorders*, 39 (2): 245–56.

Lewis, M. and Fisher, R. (2003) *Curiosity Kits*. Reading: NCLL, University of Reading.

Liberman, I.Y. (1971) 'Basic research in speech and lateralisation of language: Some implications for reading disability', *Bulletin of the Orton Society*, 21: 71–87.

Liberman, I.Y., Shankweiler, D.P., Fischer, F.W. and Carter, B. (1974) 'Explicit syllable and phoneme segmentation in the young child', *Journal of Experimental Child Psychology*, 18: 201–12.

Lloyd, S. and Jolly, C. (1995) *Jolly Phonics*. Chigwell: Jolly Learning.

Lundberg, I., Olofsson, A. and Wall, S. (1980) 'Reading and spelling skills in the first years predicted form phonemic awareness skills in kindergarten', *Scandinavian Journal of Psychology*, 21: 159–73.

Lupker, S.J. (2005) 'Visual word recognition: Theories and findings', in M.J. Snowling and C. Hulme (eds), *The Science of Reading: A Handbook*. Oxford: Blackwell. pp. 39–60.

MacCarthy, P.A.D. (1969) 'The Bernard Shaw Alphabet', in W. Haas (ed.), *Alphabets for English*. Manchester: Manchester University Press.

Maclean, M., Bryant, P. and Bradley, L. (1987) 'Rhymes, nursery rhymes and reading in early childhood', *Merrill-Palmer Quarterly*, 33 (3): 255–81.

Macmillan, B. (2002) 'Rhyme and reading: A critical review of the research methodology', *Journal of Research in Reading*, 25 (1): 4–42.

Mann, V.A. and Foy, J.G. (2003) 'Phonological awareness, speech development and letter knowledge in preschool children', *Annals of Dyslexia*, 53: 149–73.

Marsh, J. (in press) 'Popular culture in the language arts curriculum', in J. Flood, S.B. Heath and D. Lapp (eds), *Handbook on Research in Teaching Through the Communicative and Visual Arts*, Vol. 2. New York: Macmillan/IRA.

Martin, D. (2000) *Teaching Children with Speech and Language Difficulties*. London: David Fulton.

McCartney, E. (1984) 'The components of language', in E. McCartney (ed.), *Helping Adult Training Centre Students to Communicate*. Kidderminster: BIMH.

McCartney, E., Ellis, S. and Boyle, J. (2005) *The Development and Validation of Materials for Use by Classroom Teachers Working with Children with Primary Language Impairment*. Final Research Report, November 2005. Available from SLT Division, University of Strathclyde, G13 1PP.

McGuinness, D. (2006) 'Some comments on a report by Torgerson, C., Brooks, G. and Hall, J.' Available online at www.rrf.org.uk/Torgersonarticle.pdf

McNaughton, C. (2002) *Oops! (A Preston Pig Story)*. London: Picture Lions.

Medwell, J., Wray, D., Poulson, L. and Fox, R. (1998) *Effective Teachers of Literacy*. A Report Commissioned by the Teacher Training Agency. London: TTA.

Millard, E. (1996) *Differently Literate*. London: Falmer.

Millard, E. and Marsh, J. (2003) 'Sending Minnie the Minx home: Comics and reading choices', *Cambridge Journal of Education*, 31 (1): 25–38.

Minns, H. (1997) '"I knew a duck": Reading and learning in Derby's poor schools', in M. Hilton, M. Styles and V. Watson (eds), *Opening the Nursery Door*. London: Routledge. pp. 180–98.

Miskin, R. (2003) 'RML Information'. Paper given at the DFES phonics seminar in March. Available online at www.standards.dfes.gov.uk/primary/publications/literacy/686807/nls_ phonics0303rmiskin.pdf

Miskin, R. (2004) *Teacher's Handbook*. London: Ruth Miskin Literacy.

Miskin, R. (2005) *Just Phonics Handbook*. Oxford: Oxford University Press.

Moll, L., Amanti, C., Neff, D. and Gonzalez, N. (1992) 'Funds of knowledge for teaching: Using a qualitative approach to connect homes and classrooms', *Theory into Practice*, 31 (2): 132–41.

Montessori, M. (1912) *The Montessori Method* (translated by Anne George). London: Heinemann.

Montessori, M. (1964) *The Montessori Method*. New York: Schocken.

Morais, J., Cary, L., Alegria, J. and Bertelson, P. (1979) 'Does awareness of speech as a sequence of phones arise spontaneously?', *Cognition*, 7: 323–31.

Morris, D. (1993) 'The relationship between beginning readers' concept of word in text and phonemic awareness in learning to read: A longitudinal study', *Research in the Teaching of English*, 27: 133–54.

Mullis, I.V.S., Martin, M.O., Gonzalez, E.J. and Kennedy, A.M. (2003) 'PIRLS 2001 International Report: IEA's study of reading literacy achievement in primary schools'. Chestnut Hill, MA: Boston College. Available online at www.isc.bc.edu/pirls2001i/PIRLS2001_Pubs_IR.html

Muter, V., Hulme, C. and Snowling, M. (1997) *Phonological Abilities Test (PAT)*. London: Harcourt Assessment.

Muter, V., Hulme, C., Stevenson, J. and Snowling, M. (2004) 'Phonemes, rimes, vocabulary, and grammatical skills as foundations of early reading development: Evidence from a longitudinal study', *Developmental Psychology*, 40 (5): 1–17.

National Reading Panel (2000a) 'Report of the National Reading Panel: Report of the subgroups'. Washington, DC: National Institute of Child Health and Human Development Clearinghouse.

National Reading Panel (2000b) 'Teaching children to read: An evidenced-based assessment of the scientific research literature on reading and its implications for reading instruction'. Washington, DC: National Institute for Child Health and Human Development: US Government Printing Office.

Nunes, T., Bryant, P. and Olsson, J., (2003) 'Learning morphological and phonological spelling rules: An intervention study', *Scientific Studies in Reading*, 7 (3): 289–306.

Nutbrown, C., Hannon, P. and Morgan, A. (2005) *Early Literacy Work with Families: Policy, Practice and Research*. London: Sage.

Ofsted (Office for Standards in Education) (1995) *English: A Review of Inspection Findings 1993/94*. London: HMSO.

Ofsted (2001) *Teaching of Phonics: A Paper by HMI*. London: HMSO.

Ofsted (2002) *Continuing Professional Development for Teachers in Schools*. London: HMSO.

Ofsted (2004) *Reading for Purpose and Pleasure*. London: HMSO.

Ofsted (2005) *English 2000–05: A Review of the Inspection Evidence. HMI 2351*. London: HMSO.

Pahl, K. and Rowsell, J. (2005) *Literacy and Education: Understanding the New Literacy Studies in the Classroom*. London: Sage.

Palmer, S. and Bayley, R. (2004) *Foundations of Literacy: A Balanced Approach to Language – Listening and literacy skills in the early years.* Stafford: Stafford Network Educational Press.

Paris, S.G. (2005) 'Reinterpreting the development of reading skills', *Reading Research Quarterly*, 40 (2): 184–202.

Paulesu, E., McCrory, E., Fazio, F., Menoncello, L., Brunswick, N., Cappa, S.F., Cotelli, M., Cossu, G., Corte, F., Lorusso, M., Pesenti, S., Gallagher, A., Perani, D., Price, C., Frith, C.D. and Frith, U. (2000) 'A cultural effect on brain function', *Nature Neuroscience*, 3 (1): 91–6.

Peters, M. (1985) *Spelling – Caught or Taught*, 2nd edn. London: Routledge and Kegan Paul.

Primary National Strategy/DfES (2005) *Learning and Teaching Dyslexic Children.* Reference no. 1184–2005. London: DfES. Available online at www.standards.dfes.gov.uk/primary/publications/inclusion/1170961/pns_incl1184-2005dyslexia_s1.pdf

Progress in International Reading Literacy Study (2001) *Reading All Over the World.* London: DfES.

Purcell-Gates, V. (1996) 'Stories, coupons and the TV guide: Relationships between home literacy experiences and emergent literacy knowledge', *Reading Research Quarterly*, 31: 406–28.

Raz, I. and Bryant, P. (1990) 'Social background, phonological awareness and children's reading', *British Journal of Developmental Psychology*, 8, 209–25.

Razfar, A. and Gutierrez, K. (2003) 'Reconceptualizing early childhood literacy: The sociocultural influence', in N. Hall, J. Larson and J. Marsh (eds), *Handbook of Early Childhood Literacy.* London: Sage. pp. 34–47.

Read, C. (1986) *Children's Creative Spelling.* London: Routledge and Kegan Paul.

Reading Reform Foundation (2006) Various articles available online at www.rrf.org.uk/index.htm

Sampson, G. (1985) *Writing Systems.* London: Hutchinson.

Sénéchal, M. and LeFevre, J. (2002) 'Parental involvement in the development of children's reading skill: A five-year longitudinal study', *Child Development*, 73 (2): 445–60.

Seymour, P.H.K., Aro, M. and Erskine, J.M. (2003) 'Foundation literacy acquisition in European orthographies', *British Journal of Psychology*, 94: 143–74.

Shapiro, L. and Solity, J.E. (2006) 'Preventing reading difficulties through whole-class intervention'. Submitted for publication.

Share, D.L. (1995) 'Phonological recoding and self-teaching: Sine qua non of reading acquisition', *Cognition*, 55: 151–218.

Share, D., Jorm, A., Maclean, R. and Matthews, R. (1984) 'Sources of individual differences in reading acquisition', *Journal of Educational Psychology*, 76: 1309–24.

Smith, N.B. (1963) 'Historical research on phonics and word method in America', in Chall, J.S. (1967) *Learning to Read: The Great Debate.* New York: McGraw Hill.

Smith, V. (2003) 'Lifting the flaps on information', *Reading, Literacy and Language*, 37 (3): 116–222.

Snow, C.E., Burns, M.S. and Griffin, P. (eds) (1998) *Preventing Reading Difficulties in Young Children.* Washington, DC: National Academy Press.

Snowling, M. Bishop, D.V.M. and Stothard, S.E. (2000) 'Is preschool language impairment a risk factor for dyslexia in adolescence?', *Journal of Child Psychology and Psychiatry*, 41 (95): 587–600.

SOEID (The Scottish Office Education and Industry Department) (1998) *Interchange 57 Accelerating Reading Attainment: The Effectiveness of Synthetic Phonics.* Edinburgh: SOEID.

Solity, J. (2004) 'Teaching Phonics in context: A critique of the National Literacy Strategy'. Paper given at DfES phonics seminar in March 2003. Available online at www.standards.dfes.gov.uk/primary/publications/literacy/686807/nls_phonics0303jsolity.pdf

Solity, J.E. and Shapiro, L. (2006) 'An evaluation of classroom-based instructional strategies for raising reading achievements and preventing difficulties in the early years'. Submitted for publication.

Solity, J.E. and Vousden, J. (2006) 'Reading schemes vs. real books: A new perspective from instructional psychology'. Submitted for publication.

Southgate, V. and Roberts, G.R. (1970) *Reading – Which Approach?* London: Unibooks, University of London Press.

Stahl, S.A. (1992) 'Saying the "p" word: Nine guidelines for exemplary phonics instruction', *The Reading Teacher*, 45 (8): 618–25.

Stahl, S.A., Duffy-Hester, A.M. and Stahl, K.A. (1988) 'Everything you wanted to know about phonics but were afraid to ask', *Reading Research Quarterly*, 33: 338–55.

Stannard, J. and Huxford, L. (forthcoming) *The National Literacy Strategy in England – A Critical Perspective*.

Stanovich, K. (1980) 'Toward an interactive-compensatory model of individual differences in the development of reading fluency', *Reading Research Quarterly*, 16: 32–71.

Stone, B.H., Merritt, D.D. and Cherkes-Julkowski, M. (1998) 'Language and reading: Phonological connections', in D.D. Merritt and B. Culatta (eds), *Language Intervention in the Classroom*. San Diego, CA: Singular. pp. 363–408.

Stothard, S.E., Snowling, M.J., Bishop, D.V.M., Chipchase, B.B. and Caplan, C.A. (1998) 'Language impaired preschoolers: A follow-up study into adolescence', *Journal of Speech, Language and Hearing Research*, 41: 407–18.

Stuart, M. (1999) 'Getting ready for reading: Early phoneme awareness and phonics teaching improves reading and spelling in inner-city second language learners', *British Journal of Educational Psychology*, 69: 587–605.

Stuart, M. (2004) 'Getting ready for reading: A follow-up study of inner city second language learners at the end of Key Stage 1', *British Journal of Educational Psychology*, 74: 15–36.

Stuart, M., Masterson, J., Dixon, M. and Quinlan, P. (1999) 'Interacting processes in the development of printed word recognition', in T. Nunes (ed.), *Learning to Read: An Integrated View from Research and Practice*. Dordrecht: Kluwer Academic.

Stuart, M., Masterson, J. and Dixon, M. (2000) 'Sponge-like acquisition of sight vocabulary in beginning readers?', *Journal of Research in Reading*, 23: 12–27.

Styles, M. (1997) ' "Of the spontaneous kind?": Women writing poetry for children – from Jane Johnson to Christina Rosetti', in M. Hilton, M. Styles and V. Watson (eds), *Opening the Nursery Door*. London: Routledge. pp. 142–58.

Taylor, B., Anderson, R.C., Au, K.H. and Raphael, T.E. (2000) 'Discretion in the translation of research to policy: A case from beginning reading', *Educational Researcher*, 29 (6): 16–26.

Taylor, B.M. and Pearson, P.D. (eds) (2002) *Teaching Reading: Effective Schools, Accomplished Teachers*. Mahwah, NJ: Erlbaum.

Temple, C., Nathan, R.R., Burris, N. and Temple, F. (1988) *The Beginnings of Writing*. Boston, MD: Allyn and Bacon.

The Reading Agency (2004) *Enjoying Reading: Public Library Partnerships with Schools*. St Albans: The Reading Agency, available online at www.readingagency.org.uk

Torgesen, J.K. and Bryant, B.R. (2004) *Test of Phonological Awareness*, 2nd edn. (TOPA – 2+). London: Harcourt Assessment.

Torgesen, J.K., Wagner, R.K. and Rashotte, C.A. (1994) 'Longitudinal studies of phonological processing and reading', *Journal of Learning Disabilities*, 27 (5): 276–86.

Torgerson, C., Brooks, G. and Hall, J. (2006) 'A systematic review of the research literature on the use of phonics in the teaching of reading and spelling'. Research Report 711. London:

Department for Education and Skills. Available online at www.dfes.gov.uk/research/data/uploadfiles/RR711_.pdf

Treiman, R. (2000) 'The foundations of literacy', *Current Directions in Psychological Science*, 9: 89–92.

Tunmer, W. (1991) 'Phonological awareness and literacy acquisition', in L. Reiben and C. Perfetti (eds), *Learning to Read: Basic Research and its Implications*. Hillsdale, NJ: Erlbaum.

UKLA (The United Kingdom Literacy Association) (2005) *Submission to the Review of Best Practice in the Teaching of Early Reading*. Royston: UKLA.

Waddell, M. and Firth, B. (2005) *Can't You Sleep, Little Bear?* London: Walker Books.

Waddell, M. and Oxenbury, H. (1995) *Farmer Duck*. London: Walker Books.

Wagner, R., Torgesen, J.K. and Rashotte, C.A. (1999) *Comprehensive Test of Phonological Processing (CTOPP)*. London: Harcourt Assessment.

Waterland, L. (1985) *Read With Me: An Apprenticeship Approach to Reading*. Stroud: Thimble Press.

Webb, S. (2003) *Tanka Tanka Skunk*. London: Red Fox.

Wells, J. (2001) 'Phonics and accents of English: A view from phonetics', available online at www.phon.ucl.ac.uk/home/wells/phonics-phonetics.htm

Wells, T.S. (1988) *Noisy Noises On the Road*. London: Walker Books.

White, K.A. (1982) 'The relation between socioeconomic status and academic achievement', *Psychological Bulletin*, 91: 461–81.

White, T.G. (2005) 'Effects of systematic and strategic analogy-based phonics on grade 2 students' word reading and reading comprehension', *Reading Research Quarterly*, 40 (2): 234–55.

Whitehurst, G.J., Falco, F., Lonigan, G., Fischel, J., DeBaryshe, B., Valdez-Menchaca, M. and Caulfield, M. (1988) 'Accelerating language development through picture book reading', *Developmental Psychology*, 24: 552–9.

Wray, D. (1989) 'Reading: The new debate', *Reading*, 23: 2–7.

Wylie, R.E. and Durell, D.D. (1970) 'Teaching vowels through phonograms', *Elementary English*, 47: 787–91.

Wyse, D. (2000) 'Phonics – the whole story? A critical review of the empirical evidence', *Educational Studies*, 26 (3): 355–64.

Wyse, D. (2006) *The Good Writing Guide for Education Students*. London: Paul Chapman.

Ziegler, J.C. and Goswami, U. (2005) 'Reading acquisition, developmental dyslexia, skilled reading across languages: A psycholinguistic grain-size theory', *Psychological Bulletin*, 131 (1): 3–29.

Index